Metaphor Therapy

*Using Client-Generated
Metaphors in
Psychotherapy*

WITHDRAWN

'Metaphor Therapy,

Using Client-Generated Metaphors in Psychotherapy

Richard R. Kopp, Ph.D.

BRUNNER/MAZEL *Publishers* • New York

Library of Congress Cataloging-in-Publication Data

Kopp, Richard Royal.
   Metaphor therapy: using client-generated metaphors in psycho-
therapy / by Richard R. Kopp.
      p. cm.
   Includes bibliographical references and index.
   ISBN 0-87630-779-9
   1. Metaphor–Therapeutic use. 2. Psychotherapy. I. Title.
RC489.M47K67 1995
616.89'14–dc20

94-47346
CIP

Published by
BRUNNER/MAZEL, Inc.
19 Union Square West
New York, New York 10003

Manufactured in the United States of America

10   9   8   7   6   5   4   3   2

To
The memory of my parents,
Claire and Jacob Kopp,

and my grandfather,
Benjamin Sperling

Contents

Foreword

It will be appropriate to use metaphors in this foreword to demonstrate the power of this use of language.

Resistance is a common problem in psychotherapy, regardless of one's method or theoretical orientation. Those who come for therapy have two kinds of resistances: resistance *known to them* and resistance *not known to them*. Resistances that are known represent secrets so sensitive that clients consciously avoid mentioning them, thus sabotaging their therapy. Unknown resistances involve an unconscious avoidance that also can be a barrier to successful therapy.

Resistance can be compared to a logjam. Imagine huge trunks of trees coming down a swift river, moving lengthwise for the most part, rushing down the river from the forest to the sawmill. Imagine one enormous tree turning sideways, being caught by two rocks, thus jamming the passage of other logs. What can be done? One could start at the back of the logjam and remove the logs one by one until one gets to the main log. But how much more efficient it would be if one were able to remove the first log immediately! This is what loggers do: they blow up the offending log to permit the others to come down the river. And in therapy, our clients are figuratively in a jam until we get to the central issue that keeps them from living a full and free life.

Like an ant on the rim of a cup, to use another metaphor, a client can go on and on in an endless circle, exploring material that leads nowhere, avoiding clarification of the causes of their symptoms, often due to "unknown-to-them" reasons.

How does one deal with resistance? How do you get to the cause of problems? Many approaches to psychotherapy have built-in methods for dealing with resistance. Carl Rogers, for example, depended on autochthonous disclosures via generating a safe environment in which the client felt understood and accepted. At the other end of the spectrum, Albert Ellis attempts to achieve the same goal using an entirely different strategy—attacking the person's conceptions.

In *Metaphor Therapy*, Richard Kopp points out an innovative method for getting to the heart of the matter, an apparently simple one: the client and therapist, acting like detectives, look for clues to understanding the essence of the mystery by exploring and transforming the client's metaphoric language, hoping to find something that has little significance either to the client or to anyone who does not know the secret of the metaphor, but which, when the secret is revealed, becomes the key that opens the lock of the door that has stood between the person and freedom.

A related issue has to do with the concept of the *immediate moment—* an instant in therapy when one hits the nerve that controls everything, a moment of rapture, a tiny slice of ultimate joy, a shattering moment of understanding...what is known as insight, a transcendental point of change, the knife edge of moving from darkness into light or, to return to our original metaphor, the moment that the main log is removed, allowing everything to go down river.

The goal of the therapist is to help the client achieve this glorious moment of climax, but to achieve this, one must know what to do. Therapists have a variety of methods to draw on, but this well-written book offers something new and valuable.

Metaphor Therapy is above all a useful book, one in which therapists will learn new and practical therapeutic tools. Dr. Kopp skillfully presents his theories and findings in the context of a number of major systems: psychoanalysis, analytic psychology, Ericksonian hypnotherapy, cognitive-behavior therapy, Adler's individual psychology, and family systems therapy, thereby demonstrating that Metaphor Therapy is consistent with all of these and, of course, with many other systems as well. Thus, while using metaphor in therapy is an old idea, touched on by other systems, in this book the reader now has a novel way of understanding and using metaphors that extends beyond these other systems. How I wish that I would have known about Metaphor Therapy for the 50 years that I practiced counseling and psychotherapy.

I recommend this book to all counselors and therapists. Knowing how to use metaphors with clients or patients will be a magic key that opens a doorway to change.

R. J. CORSINI, Ph.D.

Acknowledgments

One of the benefits of writing a book is that it gives the author an opportunity to thank those who have helped along the way.

I am grateful to Harold Mosak, Bernard Shulman, and the faculty of the Alfred Adler Institute of Chicago (now the Adler School of Professional Psychology) for introducing me to Adlerian Psychology and the use of early recollections in psychotherapy. Adlerian principles continue to be a source of insight and inspiration in my work and in my life.

As a faculty member of ICASSI (The International Committee on Adlerian Summer Schools and Institutes) for the last 19 years, I have had the extraordinary opportunity to teach an international group of health-care professionals at the two-week Rudolf Dreikurs Summer Institute. I have learned much from their feedback and derived much from the community of caring, connection, and encouragement that is the essence of ICASSI.

Nancy Steiny and the Southern California Counseling Center provided excellent training in family therapy.

I would like to thank the California School of Professional Psychology, Los Angeles, for granting me time to work on the proposal for this book. I am also grateful to CSPP for attracting bright, caring, and talented individuals who have made my 22 years of teaching so rewarding. I especially want to express my deep appreciation to the students in my Metaphor Therapy classes at CSPP over the last 9 years. Their enthusiasm for these ideas and methods, their efforts in applying this approach in their clinical work, and their comments and suggestions have contributed significantly to the development of this approach. In particular, I would like to thank the following students who contributed case examples that appear in the first three chapters: Daniel Goldberg, Ph.D., Diane McDowell, Patricia Pulido, Terry Rattray, Ph.D., Karen Schneider, Ph.D., Joslyn Smith, Christine Welch, and especially Susan Speraw, Ph.D., who recounts her poignant work with Mike in Chapter 4.

Natalie Gilman and Bernie Mazel at Brunner/Mazel, and an anonymous reviewer provided many helpful comments and suggestions. Their interest and support enabled this book to become a reality.

Thanks to Stan Pavey, Ph.D., for his friendship and encouragement. His careful and critical reading of the manuscipt helped me express more clearly and simply what I wanted to communicate. Thanks also to Leo Gold, Ph.D., Arthur Kovacs, Ph.D., Millie Loeb, Mim Pew, Kathy and Marty Rubin, and Ira Schoenwald, Ph.D., for their influence and support.

My children, Carrie and David, continue to be a source of joy as they journey along their unique life paths. I recall the moment I first heard Carrie use metaphor as a 3-year-old, when she responded to a particular criticism by exclaiming: "Well, I did have a point!" I also have had the good fortune of getting to know the three wonderful young members of my second family–Cathy, Debbie, and David Willson. I cherish my relationship with each of them.

Finally, I am indebted to my wife and colleague, Frances Willson, Ph.D., who read every page of the manuscript and offered numerous substantive and editorial suggestions that have been incorporated into the text. As my partner in the development of the ideas and methods presented in this book, her creative contributions echo throughout these pages. As my partner in life, she has enriched my experience beyond measure.

Metaphor Therapy is a work in progess. I would welcome hearing your experiences using this approach.

Introduction

My Husband Is a Locomotive: Client-Generated Metaphors and Metaphor Therapy

KNEE-DEEP IN METAPHORS

Do you attend to the metaphors that your clients use in therapy? Are you aware of which metaphors best capture their presenting problem, their symptoms, their feelings, thoughts, and beliefs? What metaphoric language represents your clients' images of self, self-other relations, and self-life relations? Have you invited your clients to explore and transform these metaphoric representations by engaging their creative imagination, and then observed the changes that followed these brief interventions? Do you regularly attend to and use the imagery that bubbles up in your own metaphoric imagination as you sit with your clients? Earlier, when you read the phrase "knee-deep in metaphors," were you aware that it was a metaphor? If the answers to some or all of these questions is "No," then this book is written for you and your clients. You could be knee-deep in metaphors and not realize it.

BEYOND THE MIRROR'S IMAGE

Metaphors are mirrors reflecting our inner images of self, life, and others. Like Alice, we can go through the looking glass and journey beyond the mirror's image, entering the domain of creative imagination where metaphoric imagery can become a key that unlocks new possibilities for self-created "in-sight" and therapeutic change.

The impact of this journey through the looking glass is illustrated in the following case example. The therapist* invites his client, Carol, to enter the domain of her creative imagination where she explores and ultimately transforms her metaphoric image of "self" in relation to her metaphoric image of her husband. This process leads Carol to make important changes in her life.

CASE EXAMPLE: MY HUSBAND IS A LOCOMOTIVE

Carol, a 38-year-old Caucasian female, has been in weekly individual therapy for 12 weeks.* She entered therapy complaining of anxiety and depression. Carol had separated from her husband four months previously and has had difficulty adjusting to her new situation. She is constantly angry with her husband for disregarding her wishes. He has a key to the house and comes and goes as he pleases. Carol has asked him repeatedly to at least call before he comes over, but to no avail. Also, she says she knows she should look for a job but she hasn't been motivated to do so.

Carol and her therapist have discussed a number of things she could do to change her circumstances—change the locks on the doors to the house, get a restraining order to prevent further unwanted intrusions, job search strategies, etc. Carol agrees that these are good ideas and that she should carry them out. Still, week after week she comes in with the same complaints, and, when asked whether she had followed through on the actions discussed the previous week, she says that she was too busy, too upset—there is always something that gets in the way of making any changes.

During the 13th session, Carol once again complained about her husband. In the middle of her tirade, she said, "He barges into the house like a locomotive."** The therapist decided to work with the metaphor, using one of the methods described in this book. He waited for an opening and said, "Carol, a minute ago you said that your hus-

---

'I would like to thank Steve Maybell, Ph.D., for this example of his work with Carol.
"This phrase is actually a simile because the word "like" is used; the metaphoric expression would be "My husband is a locomotive." Although simile and metaphor differ in this respect as linguistic forms, they are equivalent psychological forms (see also Lankton & Lankton, 1983, pp. 78, 79).

band barges into the house like a locomotive. If he's a locomotive, what are you?" Carol responded, "I'm not sure I understand." The therapist clarified his request, saying, "Well, if you picture him as a locomotive barging into the house, how do you picture yourself?" Carol thought for awhile, and said, "I guess I'm a tunnel."

After briefly discussing her image as a tunnel, the therapist asked, "What if you could change the image so that it would be better for you, how would you change it?" Carol became quiet. She looked up at the ceiling, seemingly searching the soundproofing tiles for an answer. Then, suddenly, as if a light went on in her head, she looked straight at the therapist and exclaimed, "I'd be the derailer!"

Because they had already run a bit over time, the therapist did not have an opportunity to explore this new metaphoric image further. Also, due to the upcoming holidays, they would not meet for another three weeks.

At the next session, Carol seemed different as she walked into the office. She announced, "Well, I derailed him!" Carol went on to describe how she had gotten a locksmith to change all the locks in the house, and that she had contacted her lawyer, instructing him to get a restraining order from the court. She also sent a certified letter to her husband telling him that she would no longer talk with him because it upset her too much and that if he wanted to communicate with her he must do it through her lawyer.

How can we account for these changes, especially in light of the previous resistance? Having spontaneously created the linguistic metaphor of her husband as a locomotive, Carol, when invited to create a metaphor for herself (her "self") in relation to her image of her husband as a locomotive, created the metaphoric image of a tunnel. The empowering effect of inviting Carol to *transform* her image is evident in her choice of the SELF AS DERAILER metaphor. It appears that this transformation of Carol's self-other metaphoric image helped her to make changes she had previously resisted.

STRAIGHT FROM THE HORSE'S MOUTH: CLIENT VS. THERAPIST METAPHORS

As illustrated in Carol's case vignette, the methods introduced in this book utilize metaphors and metaphoric imagery that come "straight from the horse's mouth," i.e., spoken metaphors and early childhood recollections generated by the client. These methods are compatible with psychodynamic, cognitive-behavioral, family systems, and humanistic-existential approaches to therapy. They add to the repertoire of current metaphoric methods that emphasize therapist-created metaphors in contrast to client-generated metaphors.

WHAT IS METAPHOR THERAPY?

Metaphor Therapy is not a new "school" of therapy. Rather, Metaphor Therapy is a perspective that offers a new way of looking at current theories and methods of psychotherapy. Viewing current approaches to individual and family therapies through the eyes of Metaphor Therapy highlights their shared metaphoric properties. Metaphor Therapy emerges as a framework within which several models of psychotherapy may be integrated.

Metaphor Therapy also identifies metaphor as a specific class of therapeutic interventions that emphasize metaphoric communication between client and therapist. Specific types of metaphoric interventions found in various schools of therapy are included as members of the class. Two broad categories are identified: *client*-generated metaphors and *therapist*-generated metaphors. Two types of client-generated metaphoric interventions are introduced in this book: (1) exploring and transforming the client's metaphoric language, and (2) exploring and transforming the client's early memory metaphors. Interventions that use therapist-generated metaphoric interventions are well documented in the literature on psychodynamic, Ericksonian, and family systems approaches to therapy. Therapist-generated interventions include metaphoric interpretation (of psychodynamics, behavioral symptoms, physical symptoms, and family structure), metaphoric enactment, and metaphoric stories and anecdotes.

The theory of Metaphor Therapy rests on the proposition that individuals, families, social groups, cultures, and humanity as a whole structure reality metaphorically. It is proposed that, at an individual level, the metaphoric structure of reality is comprised of six substructures (called metaphorms) representing self, others, life, and the relations among these elements, i.e, self in relation to self, self in relation to others, and self in relation to life. At a family level, the metaphoric structure of reality involves the metaphoric structure of the family system and subsystems, and the metaphoric structure of family communication and behavior interaction patterns. At a sociocultural and transcultural level, the metaphoric structure of social and transcultural reality is revealed in language and myths, respectively.

The theory of Metaphor Therapy also proposes a neuropsychological explanation of the brain mechanisms that mediate mental (linguistic and cognitive-affective) metaphoric structures and processes. Hypotheses are suggested in an attempt to explain the neuropsychological processes underlying therapeutic changes that result from the client-focused metaphoric methods introduced in this book.

As a perspective on psychotherapy and as a classification of intervention strategies, Metaphor Therapy advances the view that metaphor is central to the process of change in psychotherapy and is not restricted to any single approach or method.

CLIENT-GENERATED METAPHOR THERAPY
AND HUMAN DIVERSITY

Developing therapeutic approaches that are responsive to issues of human diversity such as ethnicity, sexual orientation, and gender has gained increasing importance. The main focus of the research on the psychotherapeutic treatment of ethnic minorities has focused on adapting therapeutic approaches that seem most effective for each minority group. For example, Szapocznik, Santisteban, Kurtines, Hervis, and Spencer (1982) argued that Hispanic Americans, in contrast to Anglo Americans, value role-structured rather than egalitarian relationships and prefer a present-time focus in therapy. These authors hold that failure to recognize and utilize the values they describe hinders effective treatment of this population (Sue & Zane, 1987). Others have emphasized the need to appreciate the cultural values of African-Americans (Nobles, 1980; Jones, 1985), Native-Americans (Attneave, 1984; Manson & Trimble, 1982), and Asian-Americans (Kim, 1985).

Sue and Zane (1987) point out that therapists' knowledge of the general characteristics typical of various large cultural and ethnic groups may or may not impact the outcome of psychotherapy. These variables are "distal" to therapeutic outcomes, because knowledge about these factors must be transformed into concrete therapist behaviors (therapeutic strategies and procedures). For example, what is important about ethnicity is what ethnicity suggests about an individual's culture, ways of behaving, values, and experiences (Sue, 1988). Sue (1988) notes that the *meanings* of ethnicity are more important than ethnicity itself because they are more likely to influence therapy outcomes.

It is important for the therapist to avoid confounding the cultural values of the client's *ethnic group* with those of the *client* (Sue & Zane, 1987). These authors point out that, "In working with ethnic-minority groups, no knowledge of the culture is detrimental; however, even with this knowledge, its application and relevance cannot always be assumed because of individual differences among members of a particular ethnic group" (pp. 38, 39). Thus, it is important to employ specific treatment procedures that consider within-group heterogeneity among ethnic clients. Further, the therapist can establish credibility only when the client's problems are understood in a manner that is congruent with the client's *belief systems.*

The client-generated metaphoric interventions introduced and illustrated in Part I of this book help both the therapist and the client expand and deepen their understanding of the client's belief system reflected in the client's metaphoric speech and early childhood memory metaphors. There are two main ways this is achieved. First, no interpretation or external frame of reference (such as a theoretical conceptualization or the therapist's personal frame of reference) is employed during the exploration/transformation process. The therapist facilitates the client's inner search of the client's metaphoric imagery, avoiding introducing any additional content. When the therapist does offer an idea, this is done as a tentative invitation for the client to consider additional possible meanings or images. If the client rejects the suggestion, it is dropped by the therapist. Thus, clients are empowered to elaborate and change their metaphoric imagery, and therapists respect the clients' subjective experience and choices, accepting what unfolds during the exploration and transformation process.

Second, metaphoric speech is influenced by and reflective of one's culture. Because client-generated metaphors reflect the unique experience and meaning of a particular individual, the metaphor can incorporate an individual's cultural influences while avoiding broad generalizations and cultural stereotypes. Similarly, early childhood memory metaphors are images from an individual's early childhood that reflect the person's unique frame of reference, including the influence of culture and ethnicity as mediated by the family and social system in which the person was raised.

In summary, client-generated metaphors are "proximal" (in contrast to "distal") to the interaction between client and therapist, and thus should be positively correlated with positive therapeutic outcome (Sue & Zane, 1987). Further, because the process of exploring and transforming client-generated metaphors occurs *within the world view of the client*, client-generated metaphoric interventions seem especially well-suited to psychotherapy with diverse populations.

The case examples in this book illustrate the application of Client-Generated Metaphor Therapy with clients from different cultural and ethnic backgrounds (Asian, African-American, Latino/Hispanic), sexual orientations, and gender.

WHAT THERAPISTS AND THERAPISTS-IN-TRAINING WILL LEARN

This book offers "hands on" training in the use of brief therapeutic interventions designed to help both novice and experienced therapists help their clients.

Therapists will find in these pages new ways to express empathy, listen to and access unconscious processes, facilitate greater depth of experiencing and contact in the therapeutic relationship, and sharpen their ability to "see with the eyes of another, hear with the ears of another, and feel with the heart of another" (Adler, 1956, p. 135).

Newer therapists and therapists-in-training (and their instructors and supervisors) will find specific methods that can be learned and applied relatively quickly (e.g., within the time-frame of a quarter or semester). These methods also help cultivate several important skill competencies especially relevant to a therapist's development, such as avoiding taking on the "I'll fix it" role, attending to process as well as content, showing respect for and gaining an understanding of the uniqueness of each client, bypassing client resistance, empowering clients to initiate movement and change, increasing the therapist's awareness of specific ways in which his or her expectations and perspective (countertransference) can intrude into the therapy process, and developing brief intervention skills.

This book offers a manualized training approach to building skills in these interventions, including step-by-step intervention protocols. Numerous case examples illustrate these methods. The case material includes actual therapist-client dialogue, outcome follow-up in both short-term and longer-term therapy, and a diverse selection of clients who vary with respect to diagnoses, cultural and ethnic background, gender, and sexual orientation.

Experienced therapists will add to their repertoire of interventions that increase creativity and spontaneity in therapy. They also will learn a new framework for integrating a variety of psychotherapy theories and techniques, and a multidisciplinary perspective incorporating philosophical, linguistic, cognitive-affective and neuropsychological dimensions in explaining how therapeutic change occurs.

The Plan of the Book

The therapeutic use of client-generated metaphoric imagery is presented in Part I of this book, "The Creative Imagination in Metaphor Therapy."

Chapter 1, "Through the Looking Glass: Exploring and Transforming Client Metaphors," describes specific steps therapists can use to invite clients to explore and transform their metaphoric language. Case examples demonstrate the effective use of these methods, including examples showing how to anticipate and correct typical errors made by therapists as they begin to apply these methods with their clients. The names and other identifying information used in these examples have been altered to protect the anonymity of the clients.

Chapter 2, "Derailing the Locomotive: Case Examples of Brief Metaphor Therapy," describes case examples, including transcripts of therapist-client dialogue, that show how therapists can use the methods presented in Chapter 1 to empower clients to deal effectively with problems presented in brief therapy.

Chapter 3, "Back to the Future: Exploring and Transforming Early Memory Metaphors," presents a specific sequence of steps designed to evoke a memory image from early childhood that will be a metaphoric representation of a client's current life problem. Therapists learn how to encourage clients to explore and transform these early memory metaphors, yielding an experiential understanding of the relationship between childhood experience and current problems. Three case examples are presented that illustrate the use of this approach in psychotherapy.

In Chapter 4, "There's This Giant Wall Around Me: A Case Example," Susan Speraw, Ph.D., presents her work with Mike. This poignant case vividly demonstrates how exploring and transforming linguistic metaphors and early childhood memories can lead to profound, life-changing therapy.

Chapter 5, "I Think, Therefore I Am a Tea Kettle: Metaphor Therapy and the Metaphoric Structure of Reality," explores the characteristics of linguistic metaphors, emphasizes their role in the development of human language, and shows how metaphor unites the logic of words and the "analogic" of imagery. Three types of cognition are identified and discussed: logical (syllogistic/propositional) cognition, imaginal cognition, and metaphoric cognition. Results from research in cognitive psychology are discussed indicating that metaphoric cognition combines and integrates imaginal and verbal cognition. Implications for understanding how creative metaphoric imagery produces therapeutic change are discussed and illustrated, using case examples presented earlier. A theory of the metaphoric structure of individual and social reality is proposed. The term *metaphorm* is introduced as identifying the six metaphoric structures that comprise a person's metaphoric structure of individual reality: metaphorms of self, others, life, and the relations among them (self in relation to self, self in relation to others, and self in relation to life). It is suggested that the power of Metaphor Therapy may derive, in part, from the fact that its interventions access the same sensory-affective perceptual modalities that are dominant during the time when, as infants and young children, we developed our view of ourselves in relation to the world.

Part II, "Weaving the Tapestry: Toward an Integrative Model of Metaphor and Psychotherapy," discusses a variety of theories and methods of psychotherapy from the perspective of Metaphor Therapy. It is suggested that metaphor and the metaphoric structure of reality are common threads that weave the current patchwork of psychotherapies into a coherent tapestry. This tapestry, like metaphor itself, yields unifying patterns that cut across these models while preserving their rich diversity of differences. In contrast with existing approaches that view metaphors from within the framework of each particular theory, Metaphor Therapy holds that these theories of psychotherapy are themselves metaphoric structures of reality. A client's metaphoric language embodies the metaphoric structure of reality of that client, whereas theory-based interpretations point to a theory's metaphoric structure of reality. Therapist-generated metaphoric interventions are identified and discussed in relation to the client-generated metaphoric interventions introduced in Part I.

Chapter 6, "Metaphor Therapy and Psychoanalytic Psychotherapy," explores the use of metaphor in psychoanalytic psychotherapy. Client-generated metaphors are seen as integrating secondary and primary process (unconscious) thinking. Based on the observation that Freud's German term for transference (*Übertragung*) is translated through the Greek as *metaphor*, transference is seen as the process of carrying symbols and ambiguities from one time in one's life to another, from one person to another, and from one part of one's mind to another. From the perspective of Metaphor Therapy, client-generated metaphors are viewed as being direct representations of current self-object relational units that may also represent archaic self-other relations "carried over" from childhood. Several methods of therapist-generated metaphoric interpretation are presented and discussed from the perspectives of Psychoanalysis and Metaphor Therapy.

Chapter 7, "Metaphor Therapy and Jung's Analytic Psychology," discusses Jung's approach from the perspective of Metaphor Therapy. Jung's emphasis on the active imagination, symbols, and dreams is seen as consistent with Metaphor Therapy's emphasis on the creative imagination, metaphoric imagery, and the metaphoric structure of reality. The view that an understanding of archetypes and myths requires a grasp of their metaphoric in contrast to their literal meanings is discussed. It is suggested that Metaphor Therapy integrates the view that cultural myths are the narrations by which our society is unified and the view that the personal myths revealed in one's earliest childhood memories are the guiding fictions that unify an individual's personality.

Chapter 8, "Metaphor Therapy and Ericksonian Hypnotherapy," discusses points of correspondence and difference between Metaphor Therapy and Erickson's approach to hypnotherapy. It is noted that both approaches use metaphor to communicate with and activate the client's unconscious by encouraging a shift in the client's mode of processing information from primarily verbal-logical (secondary process) to imaginal-analogical (primary process) cognition. The use of therapist-generated metaphoric stories and anecdotes is discussed and illustrated with a case example.

Chapter 9, "Metaphor Therapy and Cognitive-Behavior Therapy," explores and expands current models and methods of Cognitive-Behavior Therapy (CBT). Although current CBT approaches rely almost exclusively on logical (propositional/syllogistic) forms to describe formulating a client's cognitions, (e.g., self-talk, automatic thoughts, and irrational beliefs) and cognitive schemas, Metaphor Therapy extends the concept of cognition to include the imaginal and metaphoric forms as well. Metaphor Therapy is seen as a tridimensional cognitive therapy that places CBT in a broader context. It is suggested that Metaphor Therapy offers a framework within which psychodynamic approaches that emphasize unconscious processes expressed symbolically through sensory affective imagery (imaginal and metaphoric cognition) may be regarded as different yet compatible with CBT approaches that emphasize cognitive processes expressed in self-talk, beliefs, and cognitive schemas (logical, syllogistic/propositional cognition).

Chapter 10, "Metaphor Therapy and Adler's Individual Psychology," presents Adler's view that life style is the unifying pattern of one's personality. Similarities between Cognitive-Behavioral and Adlerian therapy are discussed, including Adler's view that beliefs determine behavior and the Adlerian method of formulating the life style using logical/syllogistic cognition. Alternate approaches to formulating and working with life style are identified that emphasize imaginal and metaphoric cognition. Like the client-generated methods associated with Metaphor Therapy, these imaginal approaches access the client's creative imagination in order to heighten awareness, intensify affective experience, and facilitate insight and change. Gold's (1978, 1988) interactive approach to working with dreams and dream symbols is presented to demonstrate an Adlerian method of working with imaginal representations of life style where insight and change are stimulated using imaginal and metaphoric cognition.

Chapter 11, "Metaphor Therapy and Family Systems Therapy," discusses selected concepts and methods associated with Structural and Strategic models of family systems therapy. These approaches maintain that the family's metaphoric structure of reality is expressed through (1) verbal and nonverbal communication, (2) the family culture, and (3) behavioral symptoms and the patterned interactive sequences that accompany them. Several case examples illustrate Minuchin's use of therapist-generated metaphor in Structural Family Therapy. Strategic Family Therapy views behavior as communication that is adaptive to the family context, and thus seeks to change a family member's behavior by changing the interpersonal context to which that behavior adapts. Five ways that a person's symptomatic behavior may be seen as metaphoric of family life are identified and illustrated. It is suggested that the metaphoric structures of individual and family reality are variants of the fundamental principle that reality is structured metaphorically. Moreover, the metaphoric methods of Structural and Strategic family therapy are seen as different yet compatible with Metaphor Therapy's client-generated metaphoric interventions.

Chapter 12, "Metaphor Therapy: Integrating Individual and Family Therapy," elaborates the view that Metaphor Therapy is a framework that can integrate individual and family systems approaches to therapy. The family is viewed as a hologram—a view that emphasizes the concept of *reciprocal holism* in which the whole is seen as more than the sum of its parts and each of the parts contains the whole. From this perspective, the metaphoric structure of family reality is represented in each family member's metaphoric structure of individual reality, and each family member's metaphoric structure of individual reality is represented in the family's metaphoric structure of reality. This view is expressed in Minuchin's metaphor of the family as a ballet in which the movement in the ballet as a whole is mirrored in each of the roles and movements of each dancer, and the story of the ballet may be generated by an understanding of the movements of any of the dancers, since each moves in relation to the others and in relation to the whole. A case example is presented that illustrates how Metaphor Therapy can integrate individual and family systems approaches to therapy.

Chapter 13, "Metaphor in Mind and Brain: Speculations on the Neuropsychology of Metaphor Therapy and Therapeutic Change," discusses the possible connections between metaphoric processes in psychotherapy and two aspects of neuropsychology: cerebral hemispheric asymmetry and Pribram's holographic model of the brain. The ways in which hemispheric and holographic processes in the brain may mediate the therapeutic changes associated with exploring and transforming metaphoric language and early memory metaphors are explored.

The Epilogue, "The Pattern That Connects: Metaphoric Structure in Mind and Nature," presents Gregory Bateson's (1979) view that mind and the evolution of all living organisms in nature are unified within a single principle, "the pattern that connects," and that the pattern that connects is metaphor. It is suggested that long before humans spoke or thought in metaphor, and long before metaphor was the source of novelty and change in language and thought, nature spoke its own language of metaphor–the pattern that connects. Indeed, the metaphoric structure of reality in individuals, families, and within and across cultures may be seen as the expression in humankind of the metaphoric structure underlying the biological evolution of all living things.

PART I

THE CREATIVE IMAGINATION IN METAPHOR THERAPY

1

Through the Looking Glass: Exploring and Transforming Client Metaphors

The goal of this chapter is to present and illustrate methods for guiding clients on an inner exploration and transformation of their metaphoric imagery. Two methods are discussed. The first is used when clients offer spontaneous, spoken metaphors, the second when clients are not forthcoming with their own spontaneous metaphors.

Consider the following therapy situations.

1. A woman complains to her therapist that her boyfriend is unwilling to change, saying, "I feel like I'm hitting my head against a wall."

2. A woman diagnosed as having a manic-depressive disorder enters her therapist's office, sits down, and declares, "I feel like one of those balloons" (referring to a poster of hot-air balloons that hangs above the therapist's desk).
3. A man who is addicted to alcohol complains that his wife is not following through on things she has agreed to do. When the therapist asks if he has talked to his wife about his feelings, he replies, "I don't want to open up a can of worms."

Entering the domain of metaphoric imagery requires a shift in attention from the *logical* meaning associated with the content of communication to the *metaphoric* meaning associated with the *metaphoric image* (i.e., "hitting my head against a wall," a "balloon," "opening a can of worms," etc.). This shift invites clients (and therapists) to pause for a moment and, like Alice entering a land of wonder through the window of her looking glass, wander awhile in the sensory-imaginal world of March Hares and Mad Hatters.

A BRIEF NOTE ON THE "STEP-BY-STEP" APPROACH
TO LEARNING THERAPY SKILLS

The following steps are designed to help therapists guide their clients on an inner exploration of metaphoric imagery. They are not intended to be used mechanically, however. Whether the pace is quick or slow, whether we stop on occasion (or frequently) to rest or linger at one step or another, depends on factors such as the degree of trust present in the therapeutic relationship, the degree of psychopathology (or ego strength) of the client, the comfort level of the therapist, the timing of the intervention in relation to the psychodynamics of the client, and the time-frame of therapy (short-term or long-term).

In short-term therapy, where we seek to achieve rapid progress and resolution of a focal problem, the pace is often quick and the steps are completed in a short time period. In contrast, more difficult and complex issues addressed in longer-term therapy may require a slower pace, perhaps taking only one or two steps at a time, extending over a period of one, two, or even several sessions or more. These short-term and longer-term approaches are demonstrated in Chapters 3 and 4, respectively.

Still, I introduce this format with some reluctance, since it is evident that effective therapy can never be reduced to rigid procedures, especially an approach that emphasizes the poetics of therapy: imagery, exploration, novelty, creativity, and metaphor. Experienced therapists, in particular, may feel constrained by a structured intervention sequence. Nevertheless, I encourage you to follow these steps as you begin to use them in your therapy. My experience teaching these methods to both new and experienced therapists suggests that following the protocol outlined in this chapter (and in Chapter 3) is the quickest and most effective way to master these methods and to observe their impact. Of course, once you are familiar with this approach, you can creatively implement these metaphoric interventions in accordance with your own therapeutic style and the unique needs of each of your clients.

An additional advantage of the outlining of a sequence of steps for exploring and transforming spoken metaphors (described below) and metaphoric childhood images (described in Chapter 3) is that these structured interventions serve as manualized training procedures, facilitating skill mastery and offering a replicable procedure for empirical investigation of the efficacy of these interventions and the validity of the theoretical principles/hypotheses on which they are founded.

Use These Methods with Caution

The methods described in this and the following chapters present intensive interventions, which should be used with care and caution. For example, persons with severe Borderline Personality disorders can sometimes become extremely anxious as they explore and transform their metaphoric imagery. As with all potentially powerful therapeutic interventions, these metaphor methods require sound clinical judgment based on solid understanding of psychodynamics and psychopathology.

PHASE 1: THROUGH THE LOOKING GLASS–ENTERING THE CLIENT'S METAPHORIC IMAGINATION

Step 1

Notice metaphors! Since we are more accustomed to attending to what a metaphor refers to than to the metaphor itself, therapists have found it useful to practice listening to their own and others' spoken metaphors. With sufficient experience, you'll find metaphors all over the place (including that one).

The therapist can guide a client on an inner exploration of the metaphoric image using the following steps.

Step 2A

The therapist invites the client to explore the metaphoric image, saying, "When you say [*the metaphor*] what image/picture comes to mind?" or, "...what image/picture do you see in your mind's eye?" or, "Could you describe the [*metaphor*]?" or, "What does the [*metaphor*] look like?"

For example, to the woman with the unchanging boyfriend we might say, "When you say you feel like you are hitting your head against the wall, what image occurs to you?" It is important to use the client's words when referring to the metaphor. Note that the therapist *invites* the client to create a mental image of the metaphor. This is a crucial feature of this approach. It is the *client's* imagery that is central here, not the therapist's. The therapist guides the process by following the client as the client creates a narrative of her/his own images.

Step 2B

If the client doesn't understand the question or responds by continuing to describe or refer to the life situation instead of describing the metaphoric *image*, the therapist can say, "If I were seeing it [*the metaphoric image*] the way you see it (in your mind's eye), what would I see?"*

For example, to the woman who complains that her boyfriend is unwilling to change, saying, "I feel like I'm hitting my head against a wall," the therapist could say, "If I were seeing you hitting your head against the wall as you see it in your mind's eye, what would I see?"

If the client fails to respond to the above prompts, the therapist can ask, "May I tell you the image that occurs to me when I hear you say [*the metaphor*]?"

For example, the therapist might say to the woman mentioned above, "Well, may I tell you the image that occurred to me when you said you are hitting your head against the wall?" [*Client says "Yes."*] "Well, I saw a wall about six feet high made of bricks and you running

---

*I would like to thank Frances Willson, Ph.D., who developed this approach.

toward the wall with your head down, then hitting it and falling down, getting up, stepping back a few yards, and then repeating the process over and over. Does that fit for you or do you have/get/want to create a different image in your mind's eye?"

The therapist knows that the client has shifted to the domain of creative metaphoric imagination when the client creates a unique inner image using the language of sensory-affective imagery.

For example, the dialogue between the man (C) who complains that his wife lacks follow-through and the therapist (T) might proceed as follows:

C: We have more unfinished projects around our house than a fly has eyes. She can't seem to finish anything.

T: Have you talked to her about how you feel about it?

C: No. I don't want to open up a can of worms.

T: When you think of opening up a can of worms, what image comes to mind?

C: Umm. Well, I see them squirming out of the can and crawling all over the place.

By creating the unique image of worms "squirming out of the can and crawling all over the place," the client moves beyond the original metaphor (and metaphoric image) of "not opening a can of worms" and enters the domain of his creative metaphoric imagination. *The next step is for the therapist to guide the client on an inner exploration of the metaphoric image.*

PHASE 2: CURIOUS-ER AND CURIOUS-ER– EXPLORING THE CLIENT'S METAPHORIC IMAGINATION

Step 3

The therapist invites the client to explore the metaphor *as a sensory image.* A metaphor can be explored along the following dimensions: (1) setting (e.g., "What else do you see?" or, "Describe the scene or an aspect of the scene [*associated with the metaphoric image*]?"); (2) action/ interaction (e.g., "What else is going on in [*the metaphoric image*]?" or, "What are the other people [*in the metaphoric image*] saying/thinking/

doing?"); (3) other additional sensory modalities (e.g., "What else are you hearing, smelling, touching, tasting?"); and/or (4) time (e.g., "What led up to this?," "What was happening [*just*] before [*the situation in the metaphor*]?, "What happens next?").

In practice, usually only a few of these directions will be explored in any single metaphoric intervention. The therapist chooses the most relevant questions based on the clinical situation.

Step 4

Once the exploration of the imagery is complete, the therapist invites the client to describe his/her feelings and experience associated with the metaphoric image. For example, the therapist can ask, "What's it like to be (*the metaphoric image*)?" or, "What's your experience of (*the metaphoric image*)?" or, "What are you feeling as you (*the metaphoric image*)?"

The therapist guides the client through this process, using nonleading questions, i.e., *the therapist leads the process of the client's inner search of the metaphoric image, but meticulously avoids introducing any new content to the image.* By not intruding into the client's metaphoric imagery, the therapist allows the client to be free to create and explore the client's own image. This is crucial because questions that introduce content into the client's metaphoric image can interfere with rather than foster the client's inner exploration.

For example, one therapist invited her client to explore the metaphor I'M TRAPPED IN A CASTLE by asking, "Is there a moat around the castle?" Another therapist, seeking to explore his client's metaphor I'M SINKING IN QUICKSAND, asked, "How deep is the quicksand?" These invitations to explore a metaphoric image, although they stay within the metaphor, introduce new content (a moat) or emphasis (depth) into the metaphor. Like uninvited dinner guests they intrude and distract from using one's own creative imagination to explore the image. In contrast, open-ended questions that request additional description without suggesting what should be described invite deeper immersion into one's metaphoric imagination.

In the first instance, for example, the therapist might ask, "What does the castle look like?" or, "If I were there with you in the castle, what would I see/hear?" In the case of the SINKING IN QUICK-

SAND metaphor, the therapist might ask, "What image do you have of yourself sinking in quicksand?" or, "Describe what's happening as you sink in the quicksand?"

Exploring metaphoric images can move the client to deeper levels of experiencing. Where we seek to stimulate a change in an immediate life problem, as in brief therapy, an additional step is useful–one that can stimulate change in a client's thoughts, beliefs, feelings, behaviors, and/or relationships, especially in relation to the life-situation represented by the original metaphor.

PHASE 3: LOOKING DIFFERENTLY–
INVITING A TRANSFORMATION OF THE
CLIENT'S METAPHORIC IMAGE

When the exploration of the metaphoric image seems complete, the therapist invites the client to transform the metaphor. Since the original metaphor represents the meaning the situation has for the client, transforming the metaphoric image changes the metaphoric meaning of the situation. Even when the client's transformed metaphoric image offers little or no improvement over the original version, it can reveal important insight into the client's hopes, expectations, and degree of discouragement.

The therapist invites a *metaphoric transformation* by (1) inviting the client to change the metaphoric image, or (2) inviting the client to consider a change suggested by the therapist.

Step 5A

The therapist says, "If you could change the image in any way, how would you change it?" Let us see how the therapist might help the client explore and then invite a change in a metaphor in the case of the CAN OF WORMS.

C: We have more unfinished projects around our house than a fly has eyes. She can't seem to finish anything.

T: Have you talked to her about how you feel about it?

> C: No. I don't want to open up a can of worms.
>
> T: When you think of opening up a can of worms, what image comes to mind?
>
> C: Umm. Well, I see them squirming out of the can and crawling all over the place.
>
> T: Describe the scene.
>
> C: Uhh, let's see. I'm running around trying to catch them. I get some of them back in the can but some wriggle through my fingers. Others crawl under the furniture and stuff and are gone.
>
> T: What happens next?
>
> C: Nothing. That's it.
>
> T: If you could change the image, how would you change it?
>
> C: I guess I'd open up the can slowly and let only one or two out at a time.

The second way to invite a metaphoric transformation is for the therapist to invite the client to consider a change suggested by the therapist.

Step 5B

The therapist says, "What if the [*the part of the metaphor to be changed*] were a [*the suggested change*]?"

An example of a therapist-initiated metaphoric transformation occurs in the case of the BASKET OF WHIPS* described later in this chapter. The client, Mr. F, accepts the image of a basket of whips as a metaphor for his self-criticism and his tendency to put himself down. When he uses this metaphor again, his therapist responds,

> T: What if the basket of whips turned into a basket of teddy bears?
>
> C: Wow!
>
> T: What do you mean, "Wow!"?
>
> C: I want to dive right in, they are so soft and friendly! I can cuddle with them.

---

*I would like to thank Frances Willson, Ph.D., for this example, also mentioned on pp. 15–16.

Following this session the therapist reported that Mr. F bought two teddy bears, one for himself and one for the therapist to keep in her office for other clients to use if they wished. Five months after the session, he sent her a Christmas card with a teddy bear on the front.

Once the client has explored the original metaphoric image and transformed the image, the therapist guides the client out of the domain of metaphoric imagination, back across the "metaphor bridge," returning to the domain of logical discourse and the external world of everyday life and literal meanings. The brief detour beyond the looking glass and into the inner world of *metaphoric imagery* ends, and the implications of the journey are discussed in relation to the life situation/problem to which the original metaphor referred.

PHASE 4: BACK TO THE TEA PARTY–
CONNECTING METAPHORIC PATTERNS
AND LIFE PROBLEMS

Step 6

The therapist invites the client to "bridge back" to the original situation, asking, "What parallels do you see between your image of [*the metaphoric image*] and [*the original situation*]?" Once the similarities between the explored metaphoric image and the current situation have been discussed, the therapist asks, "How might the way you changed the image apply to your current situation?"

To illustrate, let us return to the session with the man who was reluctant to talk with his wife concerning her not following through on things because he "didn't want to open up a can of worms."

C: We have more unfinished projects around our house than a fly has eyes. She can't seem to finish anything.

T: Have you talked to her about how you feel about it?

C: No. I don't want to open up a can of worms.

T: When you think of opening up a can of worms, what image comes to mind?

C: Umm. Well, I see them squirming out of the can and crawling all over the place.

T: Describe the scene.

C: Uhh, let's see. I'm running around trying to catch them. I get some of them back in the can but some wriggle through my fingers. Others crawl under the furniture and stuff and are gone.

T: What happens next?

C: Nothing. That's it.

T: If you could change the image so it would be better for you, how would you change it?

C: I guess I'd open up the can slowly and let only one or two out at a time.

T: What similarities do you see when you compare the image of opening up the can of worms and your concerns about talking with your wife about her problems with following through on things?

C: Well, I guess I'm worried about things getting out of hand. I mean, the worms crawled all over the place and I'm worried my wife will get upset and things will be worse, so it's not worth the trouble to bring up the issue.

T: When you think of the way you changed the image, does that give you any ideas about how you might proceed with your wife?

C: Well, I guess we could try to focus on just one issue, like letting only one or two worms out and putting the lid back on the rest. That doesn't feel as scary.

CASE EXAMPLE: A TEA KETTLE THAT CAN'T LET THE STEAM OUT

Mr. J, a tall and slender 40-year-old African-American war veteran, was seen for five sessions of individual therapy while he was an in-patient in a hospital psychiatric ward. During the first two sessions, Mr. J talked mostly about his concerns at the hospital and its programs that he felt hadn't been made available to him. He was very angry and it seemed that his anger went much deeper than he was admitting.

Mr. J appeared restless as he sat across from his therapist. He was dressed in his usual "uniform," gray jogging pants and white t-shirt, his braided hair fanned out from under his railroad-style hat and over the red bandanna tied around his neck. When he talked about feeling like "a tea kettle that can't let the steam out," the therapist, a Caucasian female, encouraged an exploration and transformation of his metaphoric image. Mr. J described the tea kettle, saying it was "copper" and "very hot" and "had reached the boiling point"; there was a "plug in the spout" and the lid looked like it was "ready to blow off." When asked if he would like to change the image of the tea kettle, he said, "Yes, I don't want to explode."

Note that the therapist does not assume that Mr. J wants to change the image. The attitude is, "It is Mr. J's metaphor, not mine, so I need to first find out *if* he would like to change the image before I invite him to change it."

When asked how he would like to change the image if he could, Mr. J said that he would like to "lift the lid just a little bit and let a little steam out at a time." When the therapist asked him how he could do this in his life, he said, "I guess I could tell people when I don't like the way they talk to me or when they say something that makes me mad. That way the pressure won't build up so much."

At that point in the session, Mr. J appeared to physically relax. His breathing was less shallow and he spoke less rapidly.

Metaphoric Intervention and Cultural Diversity

The next intervention by the therapist illustrates the relevance of metaphoric exploration and transformation to issues of cultural diversity.

In another session, Mr. J talked about the way in which "people purposely put obstacles in my way" and stated that "I can't climb the ladder of success." When asked what things prevented him from climbing the ladder of success, he became vague and defensive. The therapist attempted to bypass his resistance by using Mr. J's metaphoric imagination.

T: Could you describe the ladder?

Mr. J: It's long and steep and every time I take a step someone pushes me back.

T: What does the person look like who is pushing you back?

Mr. J: (*Looking down at the floor*) I hate to tell you this. (*Pause*)

T: (*I remembered that he had once mentioned how hard it was for a Black man "to get ahead."*) What color is the person?

Mr. J: White.

T: Well, I wouldn't want to discount the effect that being Black has had on your having trouble getting and keeping a job, and I hope you will be willing to talk to me about this kind of thing.

Mr. J seemed surprised, but was able to explore this issue with the therapist. He began talking about the difficulties that he had encountered as a Black man and appeared to be more willing to establish a therapeutic relationship.

The therapist attends to the cultural issues emerging in the exploration of the metaphor I CAN'T CLIMB THE LADDER OF SUCCESS. Since these methods start with the client's metaphor and use the client's metaphoric imagination, they adapt well to working with diverse populations.

In the final session, described below, we see the cumulative effect of this brief course of therapy.

During the 5th and final session, Mr. J complained again about the anger he was feeling and began to describe his war experiences, indicating they had caused him to "shut the door to keep people out." Mr. J and the therapist then worked with the metaphor of the "door." Mr. J mentioned how hard it was to "open up" and talk about what he had been through. He then spoke about comrades he had seen die "right in front of me" and of "thinking I'd be next." He talked about learning to "follow the voices in my head" so "I wouldn't get killed," and claimed that he never got into trouble if he "just followed the voices." At this point, Mr. J admitted that he still hears voices and that was the real reason he had come back to the hospital. Looking physically tired, Mr. J said, "I'm so tired of trying to keep this secret."

At this point, the therapist discussed the need for a psychiatric consult, which resulted in a change in medication that "quieted the voices." Mr. J became more agreeable to treatment plans and created significantly fewer angry outbursts toward staff members and fellow patients.

THE THERAPIST LISTENS WITH THE THIRD EYE

There are times when it is desirable for the therapist to introduce a metaphor into the therapeutic dialogue, especially with clients who use metaphors infrequently. At such times the therapist is required to "listen with the third EYE."

To "listen with third EYE," the therapist attends to his or her own internal images and then describes the inner metaphoric image to the client. The therapist might say, "When you were talking about _____ just now, I got an image of [*the therapist's image*]. Does that fit your experience of the situation you were talking about?" This phrasing is extremely important, because (1) it shows that the therapist does not presume to know the contents of the client's inner world of meta- phoric imagery, and (2) it encourages the client to use his or her own metaphoric imagination by modeling using the content of discussion as a stimulus for evoking an internal image. This phrasing also leaves the client free to reject the image, and to replace it with one of the client's own. Thus, the procedure accomplishes the primary goal of helping the client to create and/or attend to metaphoric imagery.

Note that the therapist doesn't need to "guess correctly." The therapist's metaphoric image may be rejected by the client and the intervention can still be successful in stimulating the client to offer the client's own metaphoric image. With practice, many therapists de- velop the ability to conjure metaphoric images out of an empathic identification with the client. The example below demonstrates the use of therapist metaphoric empathy, illustrating what Alfred Adler (1956) referred to as "seeing with the eyes of another, hearing with the ears of another, and feeling with the heart of another" (p. 135).

CASE EXAMPLE: A BASKET OF WHIPS

Mr. F, a 30-year-old Caucasian school teacher, was extremely self- critical. During a therapy session in which he was, once again, putting himself down, the therapist became aware of an image—a picture that emerged in her inner stream of consciousness. She said to Mr. F, "You know, as you were talking just now, I got the image of a big wicker basket of whips sitting next to your chair and with each self-critical remark you reach in and take out a whip and beat yourself with it." Tears began to well up in Mr. F's eyes. He responded, "And I walk around with that basket strapped on my back so I always have an ample supply of whips with me."

The image of a basket of whips was introduced by the therapist and accepted by the client as a metaphoric representation of his self-critical behavior. Both therapists and clients report experiencing a deeper level of empathy when engaged in this type of metaphoric communication, either when exploring a client's metaphor or when introducing a metaphoric image that is accepted by the client.

The methods introduced in this chapter are especially appropriate to brief therapy, as will be seen in the case examples discussed in the next chapter.

2

Derailing the Locomotive: Case Examples of Brief Metaphor Therapy

In the opening chapter we met Carol, a 38-year-old woman whose husband "barges into the house like a locomotive." After transforming her image of herself as a tunnel to that of a derailer, Carol made a number of changes in her life that she had previously resisted.

In the present chapter, I will present additional case examples of short-term psychotherapy to show how brief metaphoric interventions in which clients explore and transform their metaphoric imagery can lead to insight and change.

A BRIEF DISCUSSION OF BRIEF PSYCHOTHERAPY

Though many models of brief therapy exist (Ansbacher, 1989; Budman, 1981; Davenloo, 1980; Mann, 1973; Sifneos, 1981; Sperry, 1989), most approaches share some common features:

1. The typical number of sessions ranges from a single session (Bloom, 1981) to 20 sessions.
2. A rapid assessment is made, usually in the first session, and the "focal problem" or "focal conflict" is identified.
3. Therapeutic goals are established that involve promoting change and resolution related to the identified problem.
4. Sessions are focused and structured.
5. The therapist is active and often directive, making frequent interpretations or other interventions to help the client deal with the identified problem.

The metaphoric methods described in the preceding chapter are compatible with short-term therapy. Further, these methods have some unique qualities that can play an important role in brief psychotherapy.

First, the exploration and transformation of spoken metaphors are usually completed in a relatively short time interval.

Second, the person's spontaneously generated metaphor will frequently represent an aspect of the identified problem. For example, the identified problem in Carol's therapy was her ongoing conflicts with her estranged husband, one example of which was his repeated unannounced entry into Carol's house. Carol's spoken metaphor, "He barges into the house like a locomotive," represented this conflict at several levels: (a) Carol's and her husband's personality styles, (b) the specific behavioral interaction in the situation, and (c) the circular feedback pattern in their dyadic system.

Third, the process of exploring spoken metaphors creates a pattern in pictures that parallels the focal issue. For example, when Carol created a metaphoric image of her self as "a tunnel," this brought into clearer focus her sense of helplessness in the situation.

Fourth, the intervention that invites clients to transform their metaphoric image offers an opportunity to create a change or solution to the problem in the domain of the metaphoric imagination. When Carol creates the metaphoric transformational image, "I'd be the derailer," for example, she creates a change in the image of her self as a "passive, helpless" tunnel to one of "choice and power" as the derailer. The fifth way that metaphoric methods fit well with brief therapy is that transformative metaphoric images can lead to cognitive, emotive, and behavioral changes in the focal issue represented in the original metaphor. This is illustrated by the changes Carol initiated following her "tunnel" to "derailer" transformation which altered her relationship with her husband. These changes were more congruent with her new self-image as "the derailer," and were incompatible with the "tunnel" image. Thus, through the exploration and transformation in her metaphoric imagery, Carol created an awareness that she did not have to be helpless in the face of her husband's inappropriate behavior, and that she could take action to deal effectively with him.

CASE EXAMPLES OF BRIEF METAPHOR THERAPY

CASE #1: TRAPPED IN A BLACK PIT WITH NO WAY OUT

Norm is a 39-year-old gay Caucasian male who had been HIV positive for three years. Though he had no physical symptoms, he experienced some cognitive impairment, particularly in his ability to recall recent events. AIDS dementia was ruled out. As a result of the intake assessment done at the community mental health center, Norm was referred for brief treatment for symptoms of severe anxiety, major depression, substance abuse (alcohol), and bereavement disorder.

Norm reported feeling deeply depressed for the past 10 months after Juan, a Mexican-American male who was his lover for the past 15 years, died of AIDS. Norm had drunk heavily after Juan's death. He was drinking a fifth of whiskey with one or two six-packs of beer three to four times a week when therapy began.

Norm had made three suicide attempts since Juan's death; he had never felt suicidal prior to Juan's death. He said he was experiencing panic attacks about twice a month when "reality hits me that Juan's really dead and I'm next." In addition, he reported having difficulty concentrating, some memory problems, and recurrent episodes of insomnia.

Norm is an attractive, neatly groomed man who looks his stated age, has azure eyes and thick, chestnut hair, softened in hue by a generous mixture of grey. To the world, Norm presents a persona of quiet distinction without pretention. He favors cream-colored slacks and soft pastel blue plaid shirts. The addition of a light-grey cardigan on cold days makes him look very much like a retired professor of philosophy.

Therapeutic Goals:

1. To deter him from committing suicide.
2. To reduce his depressive symptoms.
3. To facilitate the grieving process.
4. Stopping self-destructive behaviors.
5. To facilitate adjustment to HIV.

Focal Problem:

Norm will effectively grieve Juan's death and return to previous level of functioning.

Intervention:

During the initial therapy session, Norm denied current suicidal ideation and agreed to immediately contact the therapist if such thoughts should occur.

When the therapist entered the waiting room for Norm's second session, Norm stood, shoulders slightly stooped, paused a moment as if to steady himself under a great weight, and walked slowly and deliberately into the office.

N: I don't know what to do. I just sit in my chair at home, trying not to think about things but the thoughts just run around and around in my head. I can't stop them, I can't get away from them. It's so confusing. That's how I feel, confused all the time. And then reality hits me: Juan's dead. He's really dead and I'm next. I'm next. (*Pause*) I feel like I'm trapped in a black pit and there's no way out. (*Norm appeared quite anxious. He moved around in his chair as if trying to get comfortable*).

T: You feel like you're trapped in a black pit?* What is that like for you?

N: It's terrible. I don't know...it's confusing. I'm trapped and I can't get out.

T: Can you imagine yourself, for a moment, in the black pit? What are you doing there?

N: I'm (*Pause*)...I don't know. I just feel so confused about everything. When I get to thinking about things too long I just want to die. That's when the feeling comes up. When reality hits me. Juan's gone and I have nobody. There's nobody I can talk to. Juan always took care of me. Before he died, he told me he wanted me to find someone else to take care of me. He was worried about me.

Note that Norm did not move beyond the metaphor of the black pit. Rather, he described his thoughts and recollections of his present situation. Because the therapist asked Norm, "What is that like for you?" before asking him to picture the black pit and imagine himself in it, Norm responded by describing his current experience. A *direct* invitation to enter into the metaphoric image, e.g., "When you say you feel like you're trapped in a black pit and there's no way out, what image comes to mind," might have helped Norm move beyond the spoken metaphor and into the metaphoric image.

Although the therapist had a "cognitive" understanding that Norm must feel frightened and isolated, experientially getting into the black pit "with him" (seeing with *his* eyes, hearing with *his* ears, and feeling with *his* heart, as Alfred Adler [1956] would put it) helped the therapist to be more empathically attuned with Norm's subjective experience. The therapist had worried about how to get him connected up to other people. When the therapist "climbed out of the pit," the therapist didn't even have to think about what to suggest—it was almost "instinctive."

At the end of the session, the therapist suggested that Norm sit in his chair at home and talk to Juan for a half-hour each day and that he also talk to Juan's 17-year-old niece, Anita, about Juan three times a week for 30 minutes. Anita lives in the front house with Juan's mother.

---

*Norm used several metaphors to describe his experience (thoughts *run around* in my head, I *can't get away from them*, reality *hits* me, and I feel like I'm *trapped in a black pit and there's no way out*). The therapist makes a clinical decision to focus on the "trapped in a black pit" metaphor.

She had been very close to Juan, and Norm has described her as "the only person I can talk to in the family." Norm agreed to try this suggestion. He revealed that he had thought that talking to Juan had meant he was "crazy." Having the talks prescribed seemed helpful to Norm, and he left the session looking somewhat relieved.

Norm did follow through in talking to Anita and became more involved with Juan's family, in many ways taking over the caretaking role that Juan had served. Norm also recounted that Anita started confronting him on his drinking. When he told her it didn't matter, that he felt like he had nothing to live for after Juan died, Anita retorted, "That's no excuse. I lost him too, you know." Norm stated that it made him see what he was doing and it made him feel less alone.

Norm was sad at the beginning of the next session and complained of feeling somewhat anxious. When asked about the anxiety, he repeated the "black pit" metaphor stating:

> N: I don't know. I just feel trapped. Like I'm stuck in a black pit with no way out.
>
> T: That's interesting. Let's play with that image a little and see where it takes us. Can you just sit there and relax and imagine yourself in that black pit? What does it look like?

By emphasizing, "play with the image" and asking, "What does it *look like*," the therapist offered a clear and direct invitation to Norm to "move beyond" the spoken metaphor with its attendant meaning in his current life and to enter the metaphoric image of the black pit. Norm's response showed that he understood the request and that he accepted the invitation.

> N: (*Sitting back, closing his eyes*) It's just black, I can't see anything.
>
> T: What are you doing in there?
>
> N: Nothing. Just standing there.
>
> T: Just standing there?
>
> N: Uh-huh.
>
> T: What are you standing on?
>
> N: I don't know, I can't see it.
>
> T: If you were to stamp your foot on what you're standing on, what would it feel like?
>
> N: I don't know.

T: Try it and find out.
N: It's hard.

In this interchange, the therapist took a relatively active role in guiding the client's inner exploration, asking questions that were closely tied to the client's imagery. Thus, when Norm said that he was "just standing there," the therapist asked "What are you standing on?" When Norm said he doesn't know because he "can't see it," the therapist invited Norm to shift to another sense modality (stamping his feet) consistent with what Norm had already imaged (standing). The therapist phrased the question as an invitation (If you. . ., what would it feel like?) and encouraged Norm to give it a try. Though this approach worked well with Norm, it would be preferable for the therapist to take a more neutral role in facilitating Norm's exploration of his imagery. For example, instead of asking Norm what he's doing, what he's standing on, and what it would feel like if he were to "stamp" his foot, the therapist might ask, "Tell me more about it?" or "How big does it feel?" or "Do you want to find out more about the pit?" or "If you wanted to find out more about the pit, how might you do that?"

The therapist continued helping Norm define the boundaries as Norm explored the image of the black pit by slowly testing the ground, groping carefully in the dark to touch the cold walls that encircled him. As he learned the dimensions of the pit, he became a little more comfortable exploring the metaphor. At this point the therapist invited Norm to transform the metaphoric image.

T: If you could change the image in any way, would you
       want to change it?
N: Yes.
T: How would you change it if you could?
N: There'd be a way out.
T: Well, if you could create a way out of the pit, how might
       you do it?
T: (*After some minutes of silence*) Have you discovered a way
       out?
N: No...wait. I see a light. A blue light. (*Long silence*)
T: A blue light?
N: It's Juan. (*Long silence*)
T: Can you tell me more?
N: He's here, beside me, holding my hand. . .and looking

> up. (*Pause*) He's saying something but I can't under-
> stand what he's saying. I can't understand the words.

T: How does it feel to you? What do you think he's trying
to tell you?

N: That it's going to be alright...It feels comforting. It's
going to be alright. He's with me. (*Long pause*)

T: Is he still there?

N: Yes.

T: Is there anything you want to tell him while he's here?

N: (*Pause*) I want to tell him that I love him. (*At this point
Norm's voice breaks and tears begin streaming down his face.*)

T: (*Very gently*) Then tell him.

N: I love you, Juan. (*Weeping openly, leaving the image*) Why
did he have to leave me? Why wasn't I the one to go
first? It's not fair. He had somebody. He had a family
that cares about him. I have nobody...I'm all alone now.

The remainder of the session was devoted to exploring Norm's sense
of loss over Juan's death. He described Juan's final illness and death.
Norm had taken care of him throughout his illness. He was able to
express the horror and pain of watching someone he loved waste away,
the sorrow and frustration of not being able to save Juan, and his guilt
over not being able to care for Juan at home in his final three days of
life. Taking Juan to the hospital was reframed as a loving, caring thing
since Juan was no longer able to control his bodily functions or eat.
The therapist also pointed out what a loving gift he had given Juan in
caring for him (*virtually alone*) and how hard it must have been to have
to always be so strong.

Norm's experience of Juan beside him in the Black Pit appeared to
be very strong. He referred to this several times and began to create a
metaphoric image that allowed Juan to be gone but not emotionally
separated from him. He was comforted by the bond of love he felt
with Juan and said, "Just because he's gone doesn't mean the
connection's not there." He went on to recount a comforting dream
in which Juan had appeared and said that often he felt that Juan was
near to him. Toward the end of the session he began punctuating his
conversation with self-reassuring phrases stating that he "felt better."
He said that he felt he was making progress in dealing with his depression and was more certain that everything was going to be alright. He
left this session looking considerably lighter in mood.

The idea Norm has constructed of life after death based on his experience of the metaphoric image of Juan in the pit appears to have made the prospect of his own death less terrifying. He now states that he's not afraid of death, but he's not ready to go yet. He has things to do.

Note that Norm did not actually create a way out of the black pit; he discovered (created) a blue light which became Juan who was beside him in the black pit. The therapist followed Norm's lead, illustrating how the steps outlined in Chapter 1 are modified in response to the clinical situation. Since one of the main goals of treatment was to help Norm grieve the loss of his lover, Juan's appearance in the black pit clearly took precedence over the initial "goal" of trying to find a way out of the pit. Both the therapist and Norm showed courage as Norm opened himself to experiencing the feelings he had been mired in: the depth of pain, sorrow, and anger associated with Juan's death. This, in turn, facilitated the healing process and helped Norm work through his grief.

Progress toward the therapeutic goals related to the focal problem was made. Norm's suicidal feelings subsided and he expressed hope that he would have the time to do the things he needed to do. His plans for the future included wanting to travel, to visit his stepmother in another state, and to work with a local AIDS volunteer organization. He also began to work through his denial of alcohol abuse, and became active in Alcoholics Anonymous.

CASE #2: THERE'S A BRICK WALL AROUND ME AND NOBODY CAN GET IN

Bob is a 35-year-old Caucasian male war veteran who was seen for five sessions at a hospital psychiatric ward. He has suffered from flashbacks and nightmares ever since he returned to the U.S. and recalled several gruesome incidents, two of which he said he could never get out of his mind. In the first incident, he was helping to airlift some native children to a safer location when they were hit by enemy fire and the four-year-old child sitting next to him was "blown up all over me." On another occasion, he was sent out to look for his friend Buddy whose helicopter had been shot down. Bob recalled, "There wasn't enough of him to identify, but I found his glasses."

Since returning from his tour of duty, Bob had been drinking heavily and using drugs, including marijuana, cocaine, and amphetamines. He had had numerous jobs doing construction.

Bob reported difficulty controlling his anger. He was especially bothered by his inability to maintain close personal relationships, because "I'm too scared to let anyone close."

Bob told the therapist that he recently had lost his job after an argument with his boss and subsequently could not afford to pay his rent. He began "drinking myself into the ground" and finally was admitted to an inpatient ward at the hospital after threatening to kill himself, because "I've lost everything."

Therapeutic Goals:

1. To reduce and eliminate suicidal ideation.
2. To develop appropriate ways of expressing anger.
3. To help Bob enter an AA program and attain sobriety.
4. To decrease depressive symptoms.
5. To help Bob begin to develop close relationships.

Focal Problem:

Bob will begin to establish meaningful, encouraging relationships with others.

Intervention:

Bob walked into the office and sat down, attempting to put his feet up on the desk. Then he settled into his chair. Chainsmoking, he appeared friendly and quite willing to talk about his difficulties except when the subject of his war experience was brought up. At these times, he gazed at the wall or the floor. At one point, he began to cry when talking about the incident where he found only Buddy's glasses.

Early in the second session, the following interchange took place:

> B: I can't let people get close to me.
> T: How come?
> B: I don't know, I guess I just don't want to lose anybody else after Buddy. I have a barrier up that people can't get through.
> T: Tell me about the barrier?

B: It's like having a brick wall around me and nobody can get in, but I'm tired of being lonely.

T: Would you like to thin out the wall a little?

At this point Bob looked very confused and started to get away from the metaphor. The therapist helped Bob return to the metaphor by asking:

T: How would you like to change the image of having a brick wall around you?

B: I'd like to take a few of the bricks down, but only when I'm around people that I want to let in.

At this point, Bob moved on to other issues, which were addressed during the remainder of the session.

Although the therapist aligned with Bob's feeling that he was tired of being alone, she did not attend to the protective purpose of the wall. Apparently, the image of thinning the wall was threatening to Bob. A few minutes later, the therapist invited Bob to create his own transformation of the metaphoric image of the wall. Having been empowered to choose his own metaphoric transformation, Bob created a metaphoric image that allowed him to choose when and if he would take a few bricks down from the wall. The fact that Bob preferred the transformed image of "taking a few bricks down" to "thinning out the wall a little" further underscores (1) why it is important for therapists to "stay out of the way" and allow *clients* to create *their own metaphoric imagery*, (2) why therapists must take extreme care to remain vigilant about introducing any new content when guiding clients through the explore-transform process, and (3) why therapists must use extreme caution should they decide to introduce any new content into the client's metaphoric imagery.

In the next session, Bob started talking about the brick wall again.

B: I think that brick wall of mine is keeping me from being in a relationship now, but I don't want to live like this...so isolated, but I'm scared.

T: What is the fear about?

B: I live on the streets a lot and I can't afford to let the wrong person in. (*Pause*) Maybe the person I let in won't stay anyway.

At the fourth session, Bob came in and told the therapist that he was feeling less "depressed" and said that he had called his family and they were glad to hear from him, which he hadn't expected. He also called his ex-boss and apologized, explaining that he was getting treatment at the hospital. The boss offered to give him a second chance and told him he could start working as soon as he was discharged.

Bob smiled as he told the therapist these things, and then said, "I guess I'm beginning to take down some of the bricks." He continued, "I still have to be careful though. If I take the bricks out of the middle, or if I take out the wrong bricks, my whole wall might fall down and I don't want to be standing there with no protection. It took a long time to build this wall and I just can't tear it down that quick." The therapist told Bob that the wall served an important function and agreed that he should proceed slowly. Also, if he needed to, he could put back some of the bricks when he felt he needed more protection.

Recall that the "brick wall" was the unique metaphoric image Bob created to represent the "barrier" metaphor that he created when describing what was holding him back from letting people get close to him ("I have a barrier up that people can't get through").

As often happens in this work, Bob came to use the metaphor of a brick wall as an organizing metaphor for his relationships.

Bob's return visit after being discharged from the hospital offered the therapist an opportunity to assess the progress resulting from their brief work together. He told the therapist that he was continuing to attend AA meetings, which he had begun attending as an inpatient, and had gotten himself a sponsor whom "I can relate to." He was working full-time and staying with a guy he had met at work while he was saving up money to rent an apartment. He was also dating a woman whom he had met before he entered the hospital, but said, "I need to be careful not to let things go too fast. I don't want to get hurt." He smiled and said, "I've let a few people past the wall, like you and Fred, my sponsor, and I feel okay so far."

CASE #3: BIPOLAR ILLNESS IS A BALLOON

Sue, a 26-year-old mother with three children, had recently been diagnosed with bipolar disorder. Since then, her moods had begun to stabilize on Lithium. Sue felt relieved as a result of the diagnosis because she was finally medicated appropriately .

Therapeutic Goals: Subside

1. Reduce frequency of manic-depressive symptoms by providing medication education and by encouraging compliance
   with medications.
2. Increase Sue's awareness and feeling of control over these
   symptoms.
3. Identify strategies to help Sue deal with her mood swings.

Focal Problem:

Sue's manic-depressive symptoms and her feeling that they are
unpredictable.

Intervention:

Sue was looking at a poster of balloons in the therapist's office as
she talked about what it was like to finally be diagnosed with bipolar
disorder.

S: Bipolar illness is like being a balloon. Sometimes the bal-
    loon is so full of air that it is about to burst, and some-
    times there's no air in the balloon at all, it's limp and not
    pretty.

T: What does it feel like to be the balloon?

S: It's scary because when I wake up in the morning I don't
    know if my balloon is going to be inflated or not, and not
    being stable feels terrible.

T: If you could change something about this balloon, how
    would you change it? Do you even want to change it?

S: Yes, of course I do. I guess I could tie the knot on the
    bottom of the balloon tighter, to make sure nothing leaks
    out.

T: So then you would be completely stable, with no move-
    ment of your thoughts in and out?

S: Well. . .I guess that's not right, I should expect that my
    moods will be a little different every day. . .like normal
    people, right?

T: Do you feel that your thoughts should be able to roam freely in and out of the balloon?

S: I'd like to have greater control over this process and not just let my thoughts run away with themselves, like they seem to be doing all the time!

T: So how could you regulate that flow?

S: (*Laughs*) Maybe I could hire a guard to stand at the foot of the balloon and watch to see that the air in the balloon is flowing freely.

T: You said you would "hire" a guard?

S: Well, there's always a price to pay.

T: Can you afford that price?

S: I can't afford *not* to!

T: So what will the guard be doing?

S: I guess she'd stand there and either hold open the end or shut it tight, depending on what was happening.

T: So who is this guard anyway?

S: Um. . .I don't know.

T: You said "she"...Is it a female?

S: Well, right now it's the medication, but I guess when it comes down to it, the ultimate guard is really myself.

Sue became very quiet and introspective. When she spoke again she appeared very centered within herself. She seemed to be getting in touch with something deep inside of her.

Sue and the therapist sat in silence for a minute or so. Then Sue began talking about her mother, and about the abuse both she and her mother suffered at the hands of her alcoholic father. The therapist asked her what made her bring up the subject of her mother immediately after talking about the balloon. Sue replied that when she was talking about a guard being at the opening of her balloon a picture popped into her head of her mother, acting like a "guard" when it came to dealing with her father, and trying to protect her from his abuse. Sue slowly wept.

Sue reported a reduction in the frequency of her mood swings. She also felt more in control of these symptoms whenever they did begin to occur.

Here we see an illustration of the multiple meanings associated with metaphoric images. Sue's initial metaphoric meanings were that the "guard" was the medication, and then, ultimately, herself. In response to the therapist's inquiry, Sue revealed that a picture "popped" into her head of her mother "acting like a 'guard' when it came to dealing with my father, and trying to protect me from his abuse." This *automatic image* [analogous to an "automatic thought" (Beck et al., 1979)] illustrates the analogical process that characterizes *imaginal and metaphoric cognition* in contrast to the logical processes that characterize *propositional or syllogistic cognition.* These forms of cognition are discussed in detail in Chapter 5.

Sue's spontaneous association of the "guard" at the base of the balloon and the picture of her mother guarding Sue from her father's abuse also illustrates Metaphor Therapy's view that the metaphoric images created by clients as they explore and transform their metaphoric language are closely tied to unconscious memory images from early childhood. This reflects Freud's view that thinking in pictures "stands nearer" to unconscious processes than thinking in words (Freud, 1923/1960). We might also speculate that the "picture" of the guard "stands nearer" to the childhood psychodynamic influences of the manic-depressive symptoms and of the meaning Sue gives to the symptoms. These issues are discussed at length in Chapter 6.

CASE # 4: A CASTLE CRUMBLING

Ana, a 19-year-old Latina woman born in South America, immigrated with her family to the USA at the age of two. She came to the college counseling center complaining of a depressed mood and difficulties concentrating on her studies. Ana's relationships at school were poor and she described continuing family conflicts. She explained that she felt disrespected, used, and powerless when her friends would stay in her room for hours on end, not considering whether or not it was convenient for her. She added that they often borrowed materials from her room without her permission.

Ana was also distressed about her relationship with Jim and Karen. Ana was friends with Jim before he became romantically involved with Karen, and Ana and Karen have also become friends. Ana reported that, recently, she had felt "stuck in between" Jim and Karen's conflicts and she didn't understand how she got there. She was feeling used and unappreciated by both Jim and Karen.

Therapeutic Goals:

1. To improve concentration.
2. To reduce or eliminate depressive symptoms.
3. To improve relationships with peers and family.
4. To develop appropriate assertiveness skills.
5. To help Ana stop playing the role of "victim" in her relationships.
6. To help Ana develop the ability to recognize her inner feelings and needs, and to appropriately express them so that they will be heard and respected by others.

Focal Problem:

Conflictual relationships with peers and family members in which Ana feels disrespected, used, and unappreciated.

Intervention:

Ana began the 8th of 14 sessions telling the therapist about a recent incident in which she once again felt disrespected and used, and helpless to do anything about it.

> A: I feel powerless when this happens. I feel unstable, like a castle crumbling.
>
> T: Is there an image that comes to mind when you say, "like a castle crumbling"?
>
> A: Well, I see a castle that's made out of stone; it's got a tower. I see the foundation crumbling, the top is the last thing to go and it just rests on the rest of the debris.
>
> T: Why is it crumbling?
>
> A: I guess there was an earthquake or something and the foundation wasn't strong enough.
>
> T: If you could change the image in any way, how would you change it?

The metaphoric image of the castle could be explored more extensively. The therapist might ask, for example: Where are you in relation to the castle? What did the castle look like before it crumbled?

Was it occupied? By whom? Was it empty when it started to crumble? What happens now that it has crumbled?

A: I'd have the castle be made out of steel. That way, if there's a weakness in the foundation, it'll just fall over intact. It won't crumble, it can just be lifted up and be put back together.

T: So the castle isn't completely safe from earthquakes, but if one does strike, it can recover.

A: Just by being pushed back up, rather than having to be put back together, bit by bit.

T: Is there a way that this image can be incorporated into your life, being a steel castle instead of a stone one?

A: When I think of steel, I think of "invincible." I don't think I want to be that way, but I guess I can be more metal-like by telling people what I want and meaning it. I can tell people that they need to leave my room and that they can't borrow my things without asking.

Ana's eyes sparkled with an eagerness not seen in previous sessions. She giggled when the therapist mentioned this to her, saying that she was eager to go home and try out these new "things."

The therapist was also struck by the ease with which Ana came up with these more assertive responses. To an outsider, these ideas might appear straightforward, but Ana had previously been unable to adopt them. It seemed that the simple yet profound experience of seeing herself first as crumbled stone and then as a castle made of steel had allowed her to see this steel-like quality as something within her that she could express behaviorally.

The following week Ana described how she had gone home from the previous session and made signs to post on her door saying "Studying or Sleeping–Go Away!" or "Visitors Welcome." She also talked with her friends and told them she was feeling used. She was surprised by their response. They were very receptive and responsive to her concerns and feelings.

The focus of the work shifted to other issues, and Ana no longer complained of anyone taking advantage of her.

We might guess that the metaphoric image, I AM A CASTLE CRUMBLING ON SHAKY GROUND may represent deeper levels of disturbance, what Self Psychology might refer to as "fragmentation" and "disintegration anxiety" (Kohut, 1971). The short-term nature of the treatment called for a relatively limited scope of supportive therapy to restore psychic equilibrium (Muslin & Val, 1987).

In the next chapter we turn our attention to early childhood recollections, describing the procedure for eliciting a memory image from childhood that will be a metaphor for a current problem.

3

Back to the Future:
Exploring and Transforming
Early Memory Metaphors

This chapter begins with a selective review of the literature on child-hood memories, also referred to as early recollections (ERs). The goals of this review are (1) to locate the study of childhood memories within the broader field of autobiographical memory and to opera-tionally define ERs, (2) to describe the conditions under which ERs are metaphors for current problems or life situations, (3) to describe specific instructions for eliciting an ER so that the memory will be a metaphor for a current problem, feeling, and/or situation, and (4) to outline the specific steps for stimulating therapeutic change using early recollections as metaphors.

The chapter will conclude with three case examples that will demonstrate (1) how an early recollection can be used as a metaphor to explore and change a client's metaphoric structure of a current life problem, and (2) how working with an early memory metaphor can lead to changes in the client's thoughts, feelings, and/or behaviors in the present situation.

EARLY RECOLLECTIONS AND AUTOBIOGRAPHICAL MEMORY

An "autobiographical memory" is a memory about one's own life. Brewer (1986) offers a useful taxonomy identifying the three forms of autobiographical memory:

1. *Personal memory* refers to a mental image that corresponds to a particular episode in one's life, such as the time I went to a Dodger-Cub game while visiting Chicago, and Ernie Banks won the game in the bottom of the ninth inning with a home run.
2. An *autobiographical fact* is the recollection of a fact from one's past. For example, I might recall the fact (with no accompanying imagery) that I flew to Chicago on another occasion to attend a conference.
3. A *generic personal memory* refers to a general mental image. For example, I might recall what, in general, it felt like to walk from my apartment to the University of Chicago campus in winter when the wind-chill factor plummeted to more than thirty degrees below zero. This image does not appear to be of any specific moment but is a generic image of a hunched figure, pushing against an icy wind that stings my face.

It is important that therapists be able to distinguish among these three types of recall because, as we shall see, only the first type (personal memory) meets the criteria for an early recollection. Further, because it is an image of a *specific* event, an early recollection is the form of autobiographical memory that can be a metaphoric image that represents a current life situation.

An early recollection is defined as a specific, one-time incident or episode that one remembers from one's childhood and can picture in the mind's eye (Mosak, 1958). Early recollections differ from "reports" of one's childhood history. A report is a general description of childhood experiences that have happened many times. Reports lack the specific details and sequential interactions of a specific one-time incident (Mosak, 1958). Thus, while *personal memories* meet the criteria for an ER, both *autobiographical fact* and *generic perceptual memory* are considered reports.

Clients often describe "reports" using phrases like "We *used to* ice skate on the pond behind our house in the winter" or "My sister *would always* get me in trouble."

Consider these two childhood memories:

1. When I was little I used to have trouble sleeping. My father would calm me down by singing to me.
2. I remember one night when my father came into my bedroom to calm me down. I told him I was afraid because I thought I heard something in my closet. He said, "Let's see if there is anything there, you stay in bed and I'll look in the closet." He went to the closet and opened the door and looked inside. Then he sat on the bed and sang "You are My Sunshine" and I fell asleep. What I remember most clearly is the soothing sound of his voice.

The first memory would be considered a report because it does not describe a specific incident. It is not unusual, however, for clients to respond with a report when asked for an ER. When this occurs, the therapist can ask, "Can you remember one specific time this occurred that stands out in your memory?"

The second memory is a true early recollection. Note that it describes a specific, one-time incident; the actions and interactions are clearly described; and, perhaps most important, it is a clear *memory image* involving sensory imagery. It is this quality that allows us to consider the early recollection as a metaphoric image for a current life situation or problem, just as it is the metaphoric image in linguistic metaphors that conveys the metaphoric meaning of the situation to which it refers. Thus, the therapeutic effectiveness of working with

ER metaphors hinges on the therapist's knowledge and skill in identifying and eliciting a true early recollection image.

INTERPRETING EARLY MEMORIES:
FREUD, ADLER, AND EGO PSYCHOLOGY

Freud (1899/1950) saw early childhood memories as *screen memories*, i.e., the episodes recalled (by the ego) that function to "screen out" a repressed original traumatic event which, if remembered, would be threatening to the ego. In this view, what is remembered is important primarily as a potential indicator of what has been forgotten. This is consistent with Freud's structural/conflict model, the repression hypothesis, and Freud's use of free association to identify repressed material hidden beneath the camouflage of the "screen memory."

Adler regarded early recollections as the most important indicator of an individual's lifestyle (personality), because they conveyed "the story of my life" from the person's subjective point of view (Mosak, 1958; Shulman & Mosak, 1988). Like Freud, Adler noted the usual banal quality of these memories and suggested that this was due to the process of selective memory. Unlike Freud, however, Adler postulated that the mechanism of selective memory functioned in accordance with each person's unique lifestyle. Adler held that we remember from early childhood (1) only those images that confirm and support our current view of ourselves and the world (also called one's *schema of apperception*), and (2) only those memories that support our direction of striving for significance and security (also called the *law of movement* or *fictional life-style goal*).

Adlerians use ERs as projective data (Mosak, 1958) for assessing a person's lifestyle, interpreting the memories in terms of life-style constructs (image of self, image of life, image of others, image of the "fictional" goal or self-ideal of the lifestyle, and primary behavioral methods for moving in the direction of the goal/self-ideal). Thus, Adler's focus on selective memory and lifestyle emphasizes what is *remembered*. In contrast, Freud's approach to interpreting early memories emphasizes what is *forgotten*.[*]

---

*Harold Mosak, Ph.D., and Bernard Shulman, M.D., introduced me to this distinction. I am indebted to them, their colleagues in the Adlerian private practice in Chicago where I interned as a graduate student, and the faculty of the Alfred Adler Institute of Chicago (now the Adler School of Professional Psychology) for the invaluable training I received in Adlerian Psychology, particularly in the Adlerian approach to interpreting early recollections.

Like Adler, ego psychology emphasizes the role of selective memory in early childhood recollections, focusing on what is remembered in contrast to what is forgotten. The main interest of ego psychologists is the structure and function of the ego. They interpret ERs using theoretical constructs such as ego structure, defense mechanisms, ego development, and psychosexual stages (Mayman, 1968).

EARLY RECOLLECTIONS AS METAPHORS

Like spoken metaphors, ERs can function as metaphors for something else, e.g., a life situation, problem, etc. Early recollections differ from linguistic metaphors in one important respect, however. A spoken metaphor uses an image as a means of conveying the meaning of the situation to which it refers. Thus, spoken metaphors are always metaphors, whereas ERs must meet certain criteria to be metaphors. *To be complete metaphors early recollections must do what metaphors do, namely, carry meaning over from the domain of imagery (in this case, a recollected image from early childhood) to a referent situation in one's current life.*

Whether or not an ER is a metaphor depends primarily on timing, i.e., when the ER is recalled. *An early recollection that is recalled at the moment when a client is experiencing strong feelings (or symptoms) in relation to a problem or issue he or she is describing is likely to be a metaphor for that problem, issue, feeling, or symptom.*

One need not wait for ERs to occur spontaneously, however. Therapists can actively elicit the recall of an early recollection metaphor at key moments in a therapy session. But suppose the client isn't talking about anything specific or is emotionally distant when discussing a problem? In this situation, additional steps are needed that help the client move from generalities and "intellectual" analysis to focusing on a central issue, and from "intellectual" analysis to sensory experience.

Step 1

The therapist asks the client, "Where in all of this are you most stuck?" or, "In what way is this a problem for you?" or, "Which part of this is the biggest problem for you?"

After the client has described the part where he or she feels most stuck, the therapist moves on to Step 2.

Step 2

The therapist asks, "Can you remember a recent time when you felt this way? Form an image in your mind of the situation so that you begin to get the same feelings you had then—so that you actually begin to feel those feelings now in your body the same way you felt then. Use as many of your sensory modalities as you can—try to remember what you heard, saw, smelled, touched, or tasted." Allow time for the client to form the memory image and to reexperience the feelings. The therapist can check by asking, "Are you picturing the situation in your mind?" "Are you feeling the feelings in your body?" "Where in your body do you feel them?"

Evoking a sensory memory image of a recent concrete example of a focal problem or issue causes a shift from a logical-cognitive mode associated with talking about and thinking about an experience to the imaginal-cognitive mode associated with using sensory-affective imagery to directly depict an experience.* In addition, the fact that the feelings are reexperienced as bodily sensations similar to those felt in the original situation extends the sensory-affective dimension from a memory image to direct physical sensation. Creating a representation of the focal problem in the sensory "language" of the mind (imagery-cognition) and the sensory experience of the body shifts the mode of language and thought from a verbal description to imaginal depiction; from disembodied analytic thought to sensory-affective imagery and somatic experience.

The therapist is now ready to invite the client to associate to a sensory-affective image from early childhood—i.e., an early recollection. When ERs are elicited following this protocol that focuses on sensory-affective imagery, it is almost certain that the ER that is recalled will be a metaphor for the current problem. In fact, the parallels (isomorphic** structure) between the ER and the current situation may be so striking that the client sees them clearly without much assistance from the therapist. Perhaps even more important, the way in which

---

*The distinctions and relationships among logical cognition, imaginal cognition, and metaphoric cognition are discussed in detail in Chapter 5.
***Isomorphic*, meaning the same form (*iso* means "the same," *morphic* refers to form, as in metamorphosis).

the client chooses to change the memory (a method described below) can sometimes serve as a metaphoric solution to the current problem, leading to direct and immediate changes in feelings, beliefs, thoughts, actions, and/or interpersonal relations associated with the focal problem. Thus, this intervention can be useful in short-term as well as longer-term treatment aimed at more basic personality or "cognitive schema" change.

Once the client reports experiencing in the session the same bodily feelings that were experienced when the actual situation occurred, the therapist asks for an early recollection.* Following the interview procedure to be described all but assures that the recollection elicited will be a metaphor for the situation.

There are a few situations in which the therapist can elicit an early memory metaphor without going through Steps 1 and 2. In these situations, the client is already experiencing strong feelings associated with the issue being discussed and the therapist can usually begin with Step 3.

HOW TO ELICIT EARLY MEMORY METAPHORS

Step 3A

The therapist asks, "What is the first early childhood memory that comes to mind right now? Something specific that happened only once, preferably before the age of seven or eight years old" (Mosak, 1958).

This phrasing is important because clinical experience suggests that it is the first early memory image that comes to mind when the client is experiencing the bodily feeling associated with the problem situation that will be a metaphor for the current situation. Note that the client is *not* asked to recall a time when he or she felt the same way because it is not necessary for the client to be aware of the similarities between the current situation and the early recollection. In fact, asking for the same feeling or a similar situation may be distracting to the

---

*This technique is based on the work of Marlis Auterson who presented her approach to the faculty of ICASSI (The International Committee on Adlerian Summer Schools and Institutes) in 1986 in Vancouver, Canada. Her method of working with people with cancer involves asking them to focus on their bodily feelings related to their illness and then asking them for an early recollection. This approach is also similar in some respects to Gendlin's (1981) focusing technique, LeShan's (1977) work with cancer patients, and Lew and Bettners's (1993) Connexions Focusing Technique©.

extent that it shifts attention from sensory-affective imaginal processes to conscious propositional/syllogistic (logical) thought processes.

If the client offers a report instead of an ER (e.g., "We used to. . ." or a nonspecific description of a childhood experience that is not a one-time image/episode), the therapist can ask the following question.

Step 3B

"Could you tell me one time that this occurred?" or "Can you remember a specific example of this?"

These questions usually are sufficient to evoke an early memory metaphor.

If the client can't remember anything from childhood, the therapist can respond with Step 3C.

Step 3C

"Take your time. Something will come." At this point, the therapist should wait about 30 seconds to a minute before continuing. If the person still can't remember, the therapist can suggest, "It's okay if you remember something from later in your childhood, say about 10 or 11 years old or so." Wait another 30 seconds to a minute. If nothing is recalled, say, "That's okay, some people have difficulty remembering things from their childhood at first. Perhaps you will find that a memory comes to mind during one of our future sessions. Or, perhaps you will find a memory coming to mind sometime during the week at a time when you're not expecting it. If that happens, you can tell me about it the next time we meet."

Step 4

It is important to write down the memory image, using exactly the same words the person uses. The therapist inquires about the details of the memory, asking, "What happened next?" "What did you (he, she) say/do then?" "Describe it as if you were watching a play and describing what you see," until the memory is complete (when the client says, "That's all I remember about that incident" in response to the therapist's request for more details about the memory).

Step 5

Once the client has described a complete memory image/episode, the therapist asks, "What stands out most vividly in that memory? If you had a snapshot of the memory, what instant stands out most clearly in your mind's eye?" Write down what stands out most for the person, using the person's own words.

This identifies the core memory image and, in many cases, the aspect of the ER that represents most clearly the metaphoric meaning of the current problem/situation.

Step 6A

The therapist asks, "How did you feel at that moment (the moment that stands out most)?"

Step 6B

The therapist asks, "Why did you feel that way?" or "Why did you have that reaction?"

These responses help identify the metaphoric meaning of the part of the ER that is most vivid for the client.

This completes the collection of the ER.

Three questions are usually raised at this point:

1. Is it necessary to write down the memory?
2. Won't clients object or have a negative reaction if the therapist starts writing down the words instead of paying attention to the client?
3. Can a tape recorder be used instead of writing down the early recollection?

It is best to write down the early recollection as the person tells it because (1) it may be helpful to review the entire memory, (2) it is essential that the client's precise wording be recorded accurately, (3) it helps the therapist notice where more inquiry and specifics are needed.

The therapist can point out the importance of writing down the memory by saying, "I will be writing down the early memory as you tell it to me because I want to be sure to get it down the way you remember it–in your words." The therapist may also have to ask the client to slow down a bit.

Using a tape recorder in lieu of writing down the memory has several disadvantages: (1) the therapist must listen to the tape after the session, and whatever insight is gleaned must await the next meeting to be shared, (2) important material is inevitably lost in the moment of the telling when it would be most useful, (3) there is a tendency to rely on the tape recorder to remember the memory, and (4) as mentioned above, the therapist usually fails to ask for sufficient details where needed.

TRANSFORMING EARLY MEMORY METAPHORS

Recall that, from the perspective presented in this book, (1) the early memory metaphor represents the focal problem/situation the client is currently experiencing, and (2) inviting the client to change the early memory changes the metaphoric structuring of the problem/situation with the potential of stimulating a subsequent change in the client's thoughts, feelings, and actions, concerning that situation. Thus, the next step calls for the therapist to invite the client to rewrite the memory so that it would turn out the way he or she would prefer.

Step 7

The therapist asks, "If you could change the memory in any way, how would you change it?"[*] Often, clients will respond by saying that the bad thing that happened in the original memory wouldn't have happened. In such cases the therapist asks the client to "Describe what you would have liked to have happen instead. The beginning of the memory can start out the same way, but tell the rest of it as if it actually were a memory that happened the way you would have liked it to." As with the original ER, the therapist writes down the changed memory, using the same words the client uses to describe it, probing for clarity and details where needed, using Steps 3-6 as described above.

---

[*]I believe Mica Katz of the Alfred Adler Institute of Tel Aviv, Israel, was the first Adlerian to use this method. I first observed her use this approach at the Rudolph Dreikurs Summer Institute (also known as ICASSI–The International Committee on Adlerian Summer Schools and Institutes) in Austria, 1976.

Occasionally, a client will resist changing an unpleasant ER, saying, "I can't change the past. It happened that way and that's it." In such cases it can be helpful to encourage the client by saying, "True, you can't change what happened. What I'd like you to do is to create something new—a new memory. If this childhood memory were to begin as it did originally, but you could create a new image of the way you'd like it to be, how would you change it so that it would turn out the way you would like it to?"

If the client still declines to change the memory, the therapist should accept this and move on. The client's response usually suggests that the client is very discouraged and is unable to even contemplate in fantasy any positive changes in the past, present, or future, at least in regard to the issues associated with the early memory and the current problem.

There is another reason why clients decline the invitation to change a memory, i.e., when the ER is a positive memory and the client can't think of any way it could be improved. In these cases the therapist accepts the ER as an "ideal" ER. This suggests that this ER is a metaphor for how life "should" be.

The process of eliciting a metaphoric early recollection is complete when the therapist and client have completed Step 6.

EXPLORING THE CONNECTIONS BETWEEN THE CURRENT SITUATION AND THE EARLY MEMORY METAPHOR

The therapist invites the client to explore the possible metaphoric meanings of the original and the changed ER by exploring the parallels between the ER and the current problem/situation.

Step 8A

The therapist reads the ER and the changed ER aloud and then asks the client, "What parallels do you see between the memory and/or the changed memory and the current situation you focused on earlier (see Steps 1 and 2)?" The therapist empathically reflects the client's ideas.

At this point the therapist may offer additional ideas and suggestions.

Step 8B

The therapist might say, "I'd like to tell you the connections I see. Let me know which ones seem to fit for you." If needed, the therapist can go over each part of the memory, emphasizing the ways in which the memory may be a metaphor for the current situation. Focusing on verbs and adverbs will help identify the interactive patterns that are metaphoric for the current situation.

USING EARLY MEMORY METAPHORS IN PSYCHOTHERAPY

The case examples that follow demonstrate the use of early memory metaphors in psychotherapy. The first case illustrates the use of this method in single-session therapy; the second and third cases illustrate its use at different stages of long-term therapy.

CASE EXAMPLE #1: THE NOISY SLEEPER

DJ, a 33-year-old white male, has been married for almost two years. In recent weeks, DJ had begun to snore so loudly that it seriously disturbed his wife's sleep. It particularly bothered him that his wife had spent part of the night on the living room couch a few nights ago. The following transcript is taken from the middle of the single session of therapy. DJ began by describing the presenting problem in a somewhat nonchalant, humorous manner. However, as he discussed the situation in greater detail, more negative feelings emerged. Here is the dialogue between DJ and the therapist (T):

DJ:　　Well, I mean, on one hand it seems so trivial, so stupid. But, God, it could stop us from sleeping together.

T:　　That doesn't sound trivial to me.

DJ:　　No.

T:　　And I'll bet it doesn't feel trivial.

DJ:　　No, it really doesn't.

T:　　Tell me about how it feels.

DJ:　　It feels pretty bad. And the worst thing is that it's because of me, because of something that I'm doing. I mean, it's really kind of upsetting to think that I'm driving away the person I love most. And there's nothing I can do about it. I can't help it. I mean, snoring is involuntary.

T: And that upsets you.

DJ: Yeah.

T: You look upset as you say that.

DJ: Yeah, I am feeling the frustration as we talk.

DJ reports feeling frustrated as he talks about the problem, and his nonverbal behavior leads the therapist to conclude that DJ is experiencing the frustration in his body at the moment. The therapist decides to skip Steps 1 and 2, introducing the process of using a metaphoric early recollection beginning with Step 3. As we shall see, this modification works out well.

T: (*After several seconds of silence*) You know, I'd like to ask something that may sound a little funny right now. I'd like you to tell me the first early memory that comes to mind–the first memory from your early childhood.

DJ: You mean something that happened when I was a little kid?

T: Uh hmm.

DJ: Oh God, I don't know...Let's see...Anything that happened to me?

T: Uh hmm, the first early memory that comes to your mind. Whatever comes to your mind.

DJ: Okay. (*Pause*) I remember that when I was, let's see, five...maybe six...no, I was five because my sister hadn't been born yet. Fred and I–Fred is my older brother–the two of us were staying with my aunt and uncle. My parents were on some kind of vacation, and my aunt and uncle were taking care of us. Anyway, while I was there I got really sick. In fact, I came down with pneumonia. God, it was really horrible. I remember having to get sponge baths to get my temperature down, and I had a hacking cough. I would cough all night and Fred would get really pissed at me. The two of us were sharing a room. He'd keep on yelling at me to be quiet. He didn't believe that I couldn't stop myself from coughing. Anyway, at one point, he tells me if I cough one more time, he's gonna go sleep somewhere else and leave me by myself. So, I try to stop myself from coughing, but of course, within seconds I cough, and Fred jumps out of bed and grabs his blanket and his pillow and starts to leave. So I start crying and beg him not to go. I mean you know, I was feeling really sick and homesick too, and I didn't want to be left alone. But he just left, and I was all alone. (*Pause*) I guess that's about it.

T: Okay. As you think about what you just told me, what stands out most for you? If you were to take a snapshot of the memory, what would it look like?

DJ: Hmm. Just me sitting up in bed, crying and coughing while Fred is storming out of the room.

At this point the therapist should ask how the client was feeling at this moment and why he was feeling that way.

T: If you could change that memory, rewrite it so that it would have turned out the way you would have wanted it to, how would you change it?

DJ: (*Laughs*) Alright, let's see. Well, first of all, my brother wouldn't have yelled at me. Maybe he would have said in a nice way that my coughing was keeping him awake— that he knew I couldn't help it, but that it was still bothering him. Maybe we would have talked for a little while. And he would have been really understanding and sympathetic. I know. Maybe he would have gone and woken up my aunt and asked her to give me some cough medicine. (*Laughing*) And maybe she would have given him some earplugs. That would have been good.

T: And a snapshot of this scenario, the way you've rewritten it, what would it look like?

DJ: There'd be me in bed, coughing but also smiling. And my brother would be getting into bed with earplugs in his ears. And we'd both be laughing about the earplugs.

T: And how would you be feeling?

DJ: I'd be feeling good. I mean, I'd still be sick, but I'd be feeling happy inside…and safe.

T: And what is it that would be making you feel that way?

DJ: That my brother cared about me and that he was there to look out for me.

T: Hmmm. Can you tell me about how your memory might relate to the current situation that we've been talking about?

DJ: Uh hmm, yeah...I guess the snoring is pretty much the same thing that the coughing was. Well, I mean, they're different, but the effect is the same. Both are something I can't help and something that leads to me being alone. My wife left the room the other night, just like my brother did. I mean, she didn't act mad or anything, but I still felt hurt. I don't know, it was like I was being abandoned.

T: And that does hurt.

DJ: Yeah. (*Pause*) God, you know, I wonder if that's why this whole thing bothers me so much. I mean, I haven't thought about that coughing thing for a long time. But at the time, it was a big deal. It really upset me. And now this situation is so similar. It's kind of funny (*Laughs*).

T: What feels funny to you?

DJ: I don't know, I guess it's just that whole snoring thing seemed to be such a big deal. I mean, when I woke up and realized that Sandra (*his wife*) wasn't in bed with me and then I found her on the couch in the living room, I got really upset. She even said that I was making too big a deal about the whole thing. But I don't know, it like scared me.

T: It made you feel...unsafe.

DJ: Yeah.

T: You know, I'd like to read the memory back to you in its revised form—the way you would have liked it to be.

DJ: Okay.

T: (*After reading the revised version of the memory*) Does this give you any ideas in terms of your current situation?

DJ: Well...(*Laughs*) Yeah! My wife could get earplugs. I mean, it sounds funny, but it could work. We didn't think of it...Well, to be honest, we didn't really talk about it at all. I was too upset. I guess that's the main thing—we have to sit down and discuss the problem like two adults— two adults who love each other.

T: In your revised memory, you, or uh, I guess your brother, went to ask your aunt for help.

DJ: Yeah, well, I don't know. I don't really want to ask…Well, actually, you know, about a month ago I was at the doctor, sitting in the waiting room and I saw this pamphlet about snoring. (*Laughs*) This is gonna sound really dumb, but I didn't pick it up because I thought someone would see me and think that I have a problem with snoring. Well, anyway, I guess that might be worth looking into. (*Laughing*) I mean, if anyone sees me, I can just say it's for my wife.

Discussion

It is not unusual to find such clear connections between the early memory metaphor and the identified problem when this procedure is followed. However, even when not obvious to the client, the metaphoric relationship between the ER and the current situation usually emerges as the therapist and client explore the parallels between the themes in the early memory metaphor and the present situation. The reader is encouraged to test this hypothesis in the crucible of his or her own therapeutic work.

COMPARING METAPHORIC AND
INTERPRETIVE APPROACHES

Metaphors and early recollections could be interpreted from a variety of theoretical perspectives.

For example, psychoanalysts might ask DJ for his free associations, seeking to identify the latent content of the memory. Themes involving fear of abandonment and rejection, sexual themes (e.g., the sponge baths), separation anxiety, and latent homosexuality could be explored.

Although cognitive-behavioral therapists typically don't use ERs, they are ideal for identifying cognitive schemas. This approach, pioneered by Alfred Adler, uses ERs as projective data to infer one's "schema of apperception" (Adler, 1956) or "private logic" (Dreikurs, 1973), i.e., one's basic convictions about self, life, others, and the goal toward which one strives in order to feel significant and secure. While a reliable interpretation of a person's private logic requires at least several early recollections, DJ's ER suggests the following:

- Others blame me for things that are not my fault. When I try to explain, they don't believe me.
- I feel loved when I am taken care of. (He might exaggerate his need for others to take care of him and underestimate his ability to take care of himself.)
- I feel safe and secure when others are understanding and sympathetic. I feel insecure when I am abandoned and alone.
- Therefore I must try to keep others close to me and on my side, although I fear that I will do something to drive them away.

Although these interpretations might be helpful, from the perspective of Metaphor Therapy, all interpretations should be delayed until after the client has explored and identified the possible ways in which the ER and the problem situation resemble each other. There are several reasons for this:

1. Since the structure of metaphor involves creating a resemblance between two different things, identifying the points of resemblance between one's current life problem and a metaphoric memory image from early childhood identifies one's metaphoric structure of that problem.
2. The client remains in the metaphoric domain as he or she "bridges" back and forth between the metaphoric imagery of the ER and its referent situation—the current life problem. In contrast, in order to think about and talk about an interpretation, the client would have to shift out of the metaphoric and imaginal mode of cognition into a logical cognitive mode.
3. This approach utilizes the client's creativity and empowers the client to develop self-generated insight and initiate constructive changes in his/her life.

CASE EXAMPLE #2: I'M TIRED OF BEING A WORKHORSE

Lisa, a 47-year-old woman, entered therapy with feelings of depression and anxiety concerning her marriage, her poor health, and concerns about her weight. She stated that she was molested by her father for nine years, between the ages of six and 15.

The therapist described Lisa as plain-looking, appearing worn and older than her chronological age. She was significantly overweight, wore no make-up, pulled her greying blond hair back in children's barrettes, and dressed simply. She spoke in a loud, booming voice. Her pale blue eyes made poor contact and her facial expression varied between the blank stare of a lost child and animated irritability. Lisa reported that she was taking antidepressant medication as well as medication to control her blood pressure and thyroid.

At the time she entered therapy, Lisa had been married for 26 years. She described her husband as moody, depressed, temperamental, and somewhat controlling like her father. The couple had known each other since childhood and he was her first and only boyfriend after she abruptly left home at age 19 to live with relatives. Lisa and her husband were married approximately one year after their first date. Their son, aged 25, still lived with Lisa and her husband in their modest one-bedroom apartment, where he slept on the sofa. Lisa indicated that her son's social life was limited to attending technical school and attending church activities with his mother.

During the ninth session of therapy, Lisa described her frustrations with both her husband and her father, commenting on the similarities between them. Since Lisa spoke of these issues in rather vague and general terms, the therapist decided to introduce Metaphor Therapy using early memory metaphors, hoping this approach might provide some clarity and direction.

> T: So, from what we've been discussing today, what part of this would you say is the main issue for you?
>
> L: How my father always treated me like an object, like I was a possession, not a person. I was closer to my mother, but she still never showed me much attention or affection. It seemed like I was never allowed to be a kid, and since I was an only child, I really didn't know that things were so weird in my family until I had grown up. We also lived so far out in the country, without any neighbors close by, so there wasn't much to compare anything to. Looking back, I think I was just their "workhorse." All that they ever wanted me to do was to do things for them. They didn't treat me like a human being and there was never anyone to talk to about it. I had to keep everything locked deep down inside of me.
>
> T: Can you remember a recent time when you felt this way?
>
> L: Well, that's just how I feel with my husband, like a work-

horse! What happened last weekend is like what happens so often—I had to do everything around the house! I did all the cooking and cleaning and didn't get any help! It's not that I didn't want to do anything, but I was tired. I just wanted to lay down on the couch that day and have somebody do something a little nice for me for a change, but instead my husband went to (a local fast-food restaurant). He's on disability and almost every day he goes there. That's what he did that day—he went there and sat, reading his paper and drinking one cup of coffee after another. I'm so sick of it! It makes me so mad! I'm so tired of him walking all over me! I've had enough! I want a little respect and consideration!

T: Tell me what kind of sensations you are feeling in your body right now. Are they similar to how you felt then, when this situation took place?

L: Oh yes, they're the same. My stomach feels tight. I feel so tense, like I'm going to explode! If we could take my blood pressure right now I'm sure it would be way up there. And I've already got a problem with my blood pressure! I'm just so mad, it gives me a headache!

T: Tell me, what is the first childhood memory that comes to mind right now...something specific that happened only once, preferably before the age of seven or eight?

L: (*Thinks for a moment*) It was when I was around eight years old and the janitor at my school tried to molest me. I think I may have mentioned this before, but it was after school one day when I was getting ready to go home. I was walking down the hall and someone called to me from the janitor's closet. It sounded like he was yelling for help. I stopped and looked in and he was trying to get a big box down off a shelf. He was afraid that the ladder that he was standing on was going to fall. When he saw me he hollered for me to grab the ladder, so I did. Everything happened so fast after that and I can't even remember it real clearly now.

T: I can tell that this is very painful for you, but try to remember what happened next. Try to think of it as though you were watching a play. Maybe it will be easier that way. Tell me what you see and hear.

L: I know that he got down from the ladder saying that he almost fell and thanking me for helping him. Then, all of a sudden, he started looking at me differently; you know, like a dirty old man. He started saying things about my body, and then pushed himself against me, rubbing against me...up and down. It was disgusting...and terrifying! I still can't believe that I got away as easily as I did. I kicked him real hard in the shin and then just ran as fast as I could! I just kept running and running. It seemed like I ran the whole way home! That was terrible, but not as bad as how my mother reacted when I told her. That's what really hurt. I don't think that she knew that my father had done even worse, many times too, but the first thing she said after I told her about my horrifying experience was, "Well, what did you do to cause him to do that? You must have done something?" She repeated that several times. I felt so alone and hurt. What did I do? I was just a kid! I didn't do anything! Then she said, "Don't tell your father about this. Just don't tell him. Don't tell anyone. Just forget it." And that was it. She didn't comfort me or tell me how wrong the janitor had been; she never went to the school to make a report or anything. It was just like so many other things that happened in my home—it was treated like a secret, not to be talked about, and somehow I was responsible for it. I felt so alone. Nobody was there for me, but I was always expected to be there for everyone else, to take care of them. I don't feel like I ever had a childhood. I really don't know what it's like to be a kid. I wasn't given the chance.

T: Now, what stands out the most in your memory? If you had a snapshot of it, what instant would stand out most clearly in your mind?

L: How my mother reacted. I can still hear her voice saying those words over and over again. It seemed like she was always that way. Sometimes I felt more like her mother than her being mine. And I was always wrong! She never defended me. Somehow, I was always held responsible. To think that your child gets molested by a school janitor and rather than protecting her, you blame her for it! And tell her to keep it a secret! I think I lost whatever faith I had left in my mother that day. Something just died inside of me.*

T: How did you feel at that moment?

L: Terrible! What a terrible memory! I felt so alone, so hurt and dirty. I was so scared...and confused. I was really confused! I remember running to my room after that, throwing myself down on the bed, and crying for a long time. And the molestation was never talked about again.

T: Why did you think you felt that way and had that kind of reaction?

L: Because my mother acted like it never happened, like I had never told her anything. How could she have done that to me? I was her daughter; her little girl! Sometimes I don't feel that I ever had parents. They were just two people who I lived with, who I worked for and took care of, but not parents. That hurts a lot.

T: If you could change the memory in any way, how would you change it?

L: Well, of course, the molestation, like so many other things, would have never happened. But if it had to, then my mother would have acted differently; she would have protected me. I wish that she would have held me in her arms, told me that she loved me, and let me cry it all out. I wish she would have told me that everything was going to be okay and that she would have gone to my school and done something...I don't know...tell the principal and have the janitor fired or something. I just wish she would have been there for me; showed me that she cared; showed me that she loved me and that I wasn't alone.

T: What parallels do you see between the memory, or the changed version of the memory, and the current situation that you spoke of earlier?

L: Well, it's the same kind of feeling that I have with my husband–that I'm all alone. I don't get any support from him. He doesn't do anything but yell at me and at my son, or else he talks about politics because all he does all day is read the newspaper! But I don't want to talk about those depressing things. I want to talk about my church

---

*The therapist could ask, "If you could paint a picture of the something that died inside of you, what would it look like?"

and what I'm doing in school...and I want some help around the house. Why should I have to do everything? I always have to do everything, just like when I was growing up! No support! No compassion for anything that I've been through. All he does is think about himself. I know that he had a rough childhood too, but look what I've been through! And my health is so bad! I just want a little help, a little support, instead of feeling like I have to do everything and not even get a "thank you" for it. Everything's just expected, just like when I was a kid. I'm so tired of it. I'm almost 50 years old and people are still walking all over me! I just can't take it anymore. I guess I would like to change my marriage just like I wish things would have been different with my mother.

T: I'd like to tell you the parallels that I see and then I'd like for you to tell me which ones seem accurate according to how you see it. It seems like you summed things up quite well, seeing a lot of the connections between your childhood and present life yourself. And I can still hear that scared and hurt little girl crying out for help and feeling abused by yet another man. She desperately needs love and protection. And yet, your situation now is very similar to that of the past. You are still expected to take care of others, but no one is taking care of you. It sounds like you don't even have the time, or feel you can take the time, to look after yourself. You seem like a volcano about to erupt. You've been smoldering for a long time and you're about ready to blow! It sounds very frustrating and scary for you too, because you don't feel a lot of control over "how" you're gonna blow, be it physically, mentally, and/or emotionally. The little girl inside of you is still screaming to be let out and given the love and respect she never received years ago. You sound so very hurt inside.

L: (*Lisa cried for a long time. Then she and the therapist sat in silence for a few minutes before any words were said.*) Yes, that's how I feel, and as awful as it is, as awful as it "was," I feel a little better now that we've talked about it. To say it out loud feels good, like something was released inside of me. I am so tired of trying. I want things to change.

> My husband has to learn how to take care of himself more.
> He depends on me too much. And I need to have more
> time for myself, just for me. And I'd even like a little
> pampering from him. I've sure given him a lot over the
> years. If we're going to stay together, our relationship
> has to become more balanced. He has to try harder.

During the next few weeks, Lisa reported that she was much more
assertive with her husband regarding her needs and that he seemed to
respond more favorably than she anticipated. She said that he even
did some things she didn't think he was capable of doing. For example, one evening when she arrived home and told him how tired
she was, he sat down on the bed beside her and gave her a foot mas-
sage. A pleasant and intimate conversation followed. Lisa stated that
they used to have this kind of communication early in their relationship, but had not had it for a long time.

Lisa also reported that she talked to her son about the parents' need
to have some "private time" together in the apartment. They all have
agreed that two evenings a week Lisa's son would find some activity
outside the home in order to allow Lisa and her husband some time
alone.

Lisa continued to see her two doctors regarding her weight and
other health concerns. They seemed to be making progress identifying her problems and providing appropriate treatments to control them,
which resulted in Lisa feeling less stressed about her health. One of
her doctors wrote a letter to her college requesting that Lisa be granted
special consideration because of her health issues. As a result, Lisa
has been given additional time to complete the remainder of her as-
signments for the current semester.

The therapist also reported that Lisa wrote a letter to her father
confronting him about her incestuous childhood with him. Her father's
response was to continue to adamantly deny it, and to try to make
Lisa feel ashamed for ever mentioning anything. Lisa stated that, because of his poor health, she is somewhat hesitant to pursue the issue
at this time, although she reported a growing feeling that he is using
his age and medical problems as excuses to avoid the issue. Lisa voiced
her belief that her father thinks that if he puts her off long enough he
will pass away and never have to deal with the past. She added that
she was considering making a trip back east to confront him in person
when her health has improved. At present, Lisa has continued to deal

in therapy with the various aspects of her childhood molestation and mistreatment by her father and others.

CASE EXAMPLE #3: BEING SICK IS A TEST

Nora is a 35-year-old woman of Native American descent who was adopted at birth by Caucasian parents. Nora has been living with her mother and her 10-year-old son (Eddie) during the week, and her boyfriend (John) of five years on the weekend. Although she reported to her (female) therapist that her mother was ill with diabetes and needed Nora's care, her mother appeared to the therapist to lead a very active life and seemed to do well when she was alone on the weekends when Nora was at her boyfriend's home. Nora described her boyfriend as "a macho type who constantly puts me down." She often felt criticized by him, but reported that she did not challenge him.

Although she possessed attractive facial features, Nora appeared somewhat dowdy, with her head down and her shoulders slumped. She arrived for her sessions dressed in jeans, tee-shirt, and tennis shoes. Her long, black hair, which she wore parted down the middle, gave her a rather morose look.

The therapist had often observed Nora making self-deprecating statements to others in the waiting room and also to staff members. Nora feared that people wouldn't like her, and continually lamented that she had said the "wrong thing." For example, she felt she had put the staff out and that they were probably annoyed with her because she had asked for a pen to write a check to pay her therapy bill.

In therapy, Nora often asked advice from the therapist (even though the therapist always avoided offering advice) and often complained about others.

During the seventh month of therapy, Nora began the session stating that she had become ill on the previous holiday weekend while staying at her boyfriend's house. When the therapist attempted to explore the issue, Nora reported that she did not know what had been bothering her. She reported that she was distressed because she had made plans with her boyfriend to take her mother to dinner at a nice restaurant and that she had had to cancel the plans due to her illness. She indicated that she was very uncomfortable about the situation, but could not identify exactly the source of her discomfort.

N: I was so sick. I had like Montezuma's revenge.

T: It sounds pretty miserable.

N: I was really sick, but it was more than being physically sick. I'm not sure how to describe it. Something was bothering me because even though I feel like the physical stuff is gone, something feels weird.

T: I know you physically felt bad, but I was wondering if you could remember how you felt weird.

N: It was weird, like I was anxious, sort of apprehensive about what was going to happen next. It was like I screwed up and I was going to get in trouble. It happens a lot with John. Oh, just thinking about it makes me feel anxious. (*Shivers, sits on her hands, and swings her feet. Pause*)

T: Were you blaming yourself for being sick?

N: No, well...yeah. I guess so. It was the holiday weekend and I was already feeling guilty about my mom spending the weekend by herself. You know she eats T.V. dinners all week and she was looking forward to going out. I was worried that she wouldn't believe me if I called her and told her I was sick.

T: What made you think she wouldn't believe you?

N: She might think I didn't care and just wanted to be with John.

T: What if you did want to be with John?

N: Well, I wanted to, but I also wanted to take her to dinner.

T: Is that okay?

N: I don't know. I guess so.

T: You sound uncertain.

N: I feel like I need to be there for my mom because of her problems, but I also wanted to be with John.

T: It sounds like you were going to do both until you got sick.

N: Yeah, I was really sore from throwing up so much and I couldn't hold anything down. Fortunately, my son was there with me and brought me some things.

T: Things?

N: You know, like soda and crackers.

T: Where was John?

N: On Saturday, he went to work. He took one look at me, rolled over and said, "I'm glad I'm working today." (*Becomes tearful. Pause*)

T: That sounds painful.

N: It made me feel really bad, like he was disgusted with me. I hate that when he does that kind of thing. I feel like I have the plague. (*Shivers*) Now I feel that weird feeling—like I'm really nervous.

T: I would like to try and understand your feelings a little better. Will you try something?

N: Uh Oh! The last time I tried something new you made me cry. I'm just kidding—go ahead.

T: Okay, now that you have that feeling in your body, I'd like you to tell me the first childhood memory that comes to mind? Try to tell me one that happened before you were seven or eight.

N: Whoa! I'm not good at this. I don't think I remember much of my childhood. Well let me try. (*Sits and thinks*) Oh, what comes to mind is kind of gross. Well, you asked. It was Thanksgiving and I must have been about five years old. I am at my aunt's house. She had this perfect house and she didn't have any kids. There were three or four of us cousins all playing in the living room. We were waiting for the adults to come into the room so we could start dinner. Everyone was dressed up and I had this very fancy pink dress with a white smock over it. I was supposed to keep it clean all day. Well, I guess we got bored and started playing tag. At first, we were just fooling around and sort of grabbing at each other, but somehow we started running. I tripped over the foot of one of my cousins—I hit a glass table and cut my forehead open. Everyone started yelling. I didn't though because I got scared. My aunt came into the room and started yelling, "Get her out of here, she's getting blood all over the carpet." The carpet was white—I can see it right now and it was all covered with red. My aunt was furious; her face was all red. My mom was trying to clean it up and wasn't saying much. Then my dad came into the room and carried me out to the car. He held a cloth on my head and drove with the other hand to the hospital. Then he sat with me in the emergency room. I was feeling really nervous because I felt like I had ruined my aunt's carpet and my new dress. I knew my aunt and my mom were going to be really mad, but then my dad told me not to worry. He was holding a cloth on my head and waiting for the doctor. He just sat there holding my hand.

T: How did you feel?

N: I felt really nervous on the way to the hospital 'cause I felt like I ruined everyone's day, but then in the car with my dad I started feeling safe and okay. I felt like he loved me and he would somehow fix my aunt's carpet and make it okay so she wouldn't be mad anymore.

T: Do you remember anyone else in the picture?

N: No, I just remember my aunt and my mom being mad, my cousins screaming and my dad taking care of me.

T: What stands out most for you in the memory?

N: Well, really, it's like two things—the blood on the carpet and my dad holding my hand. Actually, I think it is my dad holding my hand.

T: How did you feel?

N: Like I was safe and that he would protect me. He could always make me feel that way. I realized he wasn't angry with me and that he cared.

T: If you could change the memory in any way, how would you change it?

N: Well, I guess I wouldn't have been playing tag and gotten hurt, but I don't know, I wouldn't want to change my dad holding my hand because I felt special and that he loved me. I was always close to my dad, and he treated me like I was special. (*Pauses*)*

T: What connections do you see between this memory and the situation over the weekend?

N: (*Thinks, then smiles*) Well, I guess I wished that John would have taken care of me. It seems like he can't be bothered and that he actually gets angry with me. I felt like he didn't really care. He always gets mad if I am sick, and I always have this feeling. I think he loses patience with me.

---

*The therapist might ask, "Are there any changes you would make in the memory regarding your mother?"

T: So this has happened before?

N: Yeah, sometimes I think I like to get sick. (*Long pause*)

T: Do you have any thoughts about what this is about?

N: I'm beginning to think this is like a test.

T: And John fails all the time?

N: I guess I want to know if he cares. I feel like I need him to show me some signs of affection, and when I'm sick he doesn't give me anything. Well, he gives me less than usual—which isn't much.

Nora continued to talk to the therapist about her relationship with John and her need for someone to take care of her. She also cried a great deal as she discussed other failed relationships with men due to their mistreatment of her son. However, she also reported that she did not really feel like anyone cared about her since her father who had died four years ago. Although she had talked about missing her dad in previous sessions, in this session she developed some insight into the role her father played in her life and related her current situation to her early memory in which her father took care of her.

In the next session, Nora reported that she was really dissatisfied with her relationship with John, and also stated that she was bothered by the fact that John is years older than her. Further exploration led Nora to recognize that she viewed John as a father figure and that she continually expected him to care for her. She also lamented that she had given up all of her hobbies during their five-year relationship because "all he likes to do is watch T.V." Two weeks after Nora explored and transformed her early memory metaphor, she reported to the therapist that she had called her boyfriend and broken off the relationship. While she had been complaining throughout the treatment that she was very unhappy with his behavior toward her and her son, Nora had also said that she felt trapped. She had confronted him on many occasions about his treatment of her son, but she stated that her complaints had not registered with him. This time, however, when John informed her that he had no intention of changing, Nora decided to end the relationship.

Nora reported feeling very relieved and that she had realized that she could no longer live with John's behavior. She also reported that she did not want to count on his ability to change, so she had made plans to become involved with different activities. Moreover, Nora said she decided that, from now on, her son would have a higher priority in her life. She indicated that her relationship with her son had improved greatly, and that his bouts of enuresis had ceased.* The therapist also noted that Nora's interactions with her son had become significantly more positive and that he had been less defiant with her. Finally, Nora stated that she had gone out to lunch with co-workers several times during the past three weeks.

EARLY MEMORY METAPHORS AS PERSONAL MYTH

Rollo May (1991) stresses the central importance of myth in human experience, noting that "the myth of a given person can often be discerned with a particular clarity in [that person's] earliest childhood memories" (p. 65), and that "Memory and myth are inseparable. . ." (p. 70).** Thus, the three cases presented above may be viewed as illustrating how Metaphor Therapy enables clients to access their personal myths to understand and potentially change themselves and their lives.

---

*It is difficult to determine at this point whether the cessation of episodes of enuresis is due to the improved relationship between Nora and her son, or to the fact that John has left, and the son is now without a male competitor for his mother's attention, or a combination of these (and/or other) factors.
**This theme will be explored in greater depth in Chapter 7.

4

There's This Giant Wall Around Me: A Case Example

Susan Speraw, Ph.D.*

Mike was seen over the course of one year for a total of 70 sessions. Except for brief periods of crisis when Mike was seen twice a week, 50-minute sessions were held weekly.

BACKGROUND

The first time I saw "Mike" I was struck by his fragile appearance. Tall in stature, but delicate in body build, he stood before me in the

*Susan Speraw, Ph.D., R.N., is Director of the Division of Pediatric Psychology at T. C. Thompson Children's Hospital Medical Center, Chattanooga, Tennessee, and Assistant Professor of Pediatrics at the University of Tennessee College of Medicine, Chattanooga.

lobby smiling weakly through dry, cracked lips that were pale and trembling. His skin was creamy white, with gaunt cheeks flushed bright red. As we shook hands for the first time his grip was strong despite the presence of a slight tremor which was noticeable when his hand was extended. His thin face and watery-blue eyes were framed by black hair worn slightly spiked upward in a subdued but noticeably contemporary style, and a single small diamond stud earring glistened in his left earlobe. He was wearing pastel shorts and a black shirt which was cut so full as to look more like a blouse. He carried over his shoulder a large multicolored woven bag with a fringe along the bottom. He clutched it securely throughout the first session, sometimes holding on so tightly that his knuckles turned white. Mike always spoke softly, but he was articulate and his affect was appropriate. His eye contact was good and he was generally very engaged in the therapy process.

The family history that Mike presented was complex. He originally stated that he was the older of two children. His younger brother was 15 years old and the natural child of his parents. Presently 21 years old, Mike had always known that he was adopted. One year ago, after a search of several years, Mike contacted his birth father and the two had developed a strong relationship. Mike was seeing his birth father twice a week, but was constantly worried that he could be abandoned again if he did anything to displease him. Mike's adoptive father was a prominent professional and a recovering alcoholic. According to Mike, during the years when he was growing up his adoptive father was almost always drunk and never available to his growing sons. It had only been within the past two years, after coming to the brink of financial ruin, that his father had attempted to control his drinking. Alcoholism was not his father's only problem, however. On a daily basis throughout his entire life Mike has been exposed to, and asked to "share" with his father, pornographic movies, videos, magazines and assorted sexual paraphernalia. In addition, Mike was often witness to his father's acting out of aberrant sexual behavior and sadomasochistic sexual acts between his parents.

Mike's mother was also a professional. Although he expressed feeling closer to her than to his father, Mike said that his mother loved him "too much." He had no actual memories of any sexual molestation as a child, but he was able to recall his family playing nude games in the swimming pool when he was eight or 10 years of age. Those "games" disturbed him very much and he recalled trying to avoid swimming as a child, although his parents always coerced him into the water. The relationship between Mike's parents had always been poor. He remembered that when his father was drunk he was very abusive to his mother and often beat her. He did not recall being beaten himself. At the time of the first session, Mike's parents had been divorced for two years and Mike was living with his mother and brother.

His brother is a concern for Mike. He reported worrying about him all the time and was afraid to leave his brother alone with either of his adoptive parents. During the initial therapy sessions, Mike never mentioned the existence of any other immediate family member.

Mike stated that the primary reason he had decided to seek treatment was to come to terms with his homosexuality so that he could "say I'm gay without throwing up." He also was hoping for some assistance in resolving a three-year problem with agoraphobia and panic, and in coping with persistent feelings of dread and anxiety that accompanied the coming of night and the act of going to sleep. Mike said that he needed help to find out who he was and to eventually come to like himself as a person. He was confused about his gender, fearful of venturing far from home, and afraid of dying when he was at home. He was also very lonely, and expressed feelings of desolation over having no friends or peers with whom he could relate. He could not recall ever having had a good friend. He stated that for his entire life he had always been an outsider, and perceived by others as being different. During his school years, he had often been the object of ridicule among his classmates.

Mike first became acutely aware of his gender identification conflicts when he began noticing body changes associated with puberty at about the age of 11. He recalled being extremely upset by the development of secondary sex characteristics such as a deepening voice and a male pattern of hair distribution. By the age of 13, Mike had given up attempting to shave off his body hair and instead resorted to showering fully clothed to avoid having to look at his body, a practice which had continued up to the time he presented for therapy. In addition, Mike kept all the mirrors in his room covered with sheeting so he would not have to look at himself. Mike remembered the age of 15 as being very traumatic. During that year, he began wearing heavy make-up to cover his facial hair and enhance his appearance, long hair pieces, flashy jewelry, and girls' blouses. He was aware at that time of wanting boys to notice him and think he was pretty. His appearance caused quite a disturbance at home and he ran away briefly to avoid arguing with his parents about his cross-dressing.

Just barely 17, Mike had his first homosexual intimate relationship. Though brief, it was intense. After three weeks of daily sexual activity, Mike discovered that he had contracted a sexually transmitted disease, and the relationship ended. Even though he was successfully treated, in his mind he was certain that he had contracted a fatal disease and would die soon. He lived with the specter of death every day for months until he was medically examined and assured that he was healthy and disease-free. For the next three years Mike avoided all other intimate relationships and vowed never to make his homosexuality known. At one time, he did attempt to confess his sexual orientation to his mother, but she ignored him and continued to talk about him marrying. His adoptive father had no idea that he was gay, and Mike could not foresee a time when he would want to tell him. His natural father was a known "gay basher" who harbored the opinion that "all gays should be shot," so Mike was terrified that he would find out and abandon him again. Mike expressed hatred for his homosexuality and spoke of times when he "tried to be heterosexual" with no success. He spoke poignantly of praying to God every day to make him not be gay, and was disheartened to think that his prayers might be futile. Therefore, he expressed the wish that through therapy he might eventually come to accept himself. He stated that if he could not come to that acceptance, he believed that suicide was his only option for obtaining inner peace.

Mike's problems with agoraphobia and panic had begun three years ago when he had his first and last experience with marijuana. Under the influence of the drug, he felt himself out of control and feared dying. Since that first terror-filled experience, he had endured similar episodes of panic and agoraphobic feelings, usually at times when he felt himself out of control (such as spinning while dancing, or becoming lost on an unfamiliar highway). He had been treated with Xanax and Buspar in the past and was currently on a maintenance dose of Norpramin which he believed to be of some benefit to him. He remained afraid to leave home, however, and in recent years had found that his comfort zone away from home had become increasingly constricted.

Mike's sleep problems had been ongoing for many years, at least since early adolescence. Beginning with dusk, he experienced somatic sensations of "coldness" in the pit of his stomach, nervousness, and a sense of impending doom. By bedtime, he was usually terrified that he would die and experienced fantasies of his heart stopping and his body turning blue, only to be discovered dead by his mother hours later. He feared that these fantasies were premonitions of the way he would ultimately die.

Although Mike was able to maintain a job as a clerk in a store, his occupation did little to tap his creative talents or genuine interests. Privately, he lived the life of a poet and artist, writing and painting in solitude, not sharing his work with others. His art and creativity would ultimately provide valuable keys to his interior life and struggles, and would furnish the bridge through which he could escape his inner turmoil.

THERE'S THIS GIANT WALL AROUND ME

At our first meeting, Mike exhibited symptoms of major depression. The night before the session he had a particularly difficult time getting to sleep and said that his feelings of isolation were as intense as they had ever been. After providing some personal history, Mike voiced the belief that ultimately he would have to commit suicide in order to end the pain of his loneliness and fear. He denied any present desire to commit suicide. In this initial session, Mike introduced the first of many metaphors: the metaphor of a wall. Although our metaphorical exchange was brief, it had a powerful effect which endured through the session:

> M: Last night I thought about it again—about suicide. I don't know why. I'm so afraid to die. It's just that there is this giant wall around me…Oh, I don't know.
>
> T: Tell me about that wall.
>
> M: There's not much to tell. It's all around me. I shout and shout, but nobody hears me! Oh, why am I here; it's all so futile anyway. I can't push the wall away. There's no way to get rid of it. Can coming here help me get rid of the wall?
>
> T: Maybe we don't have to get rid of it. What if we were able to help you find a way to put a door in it?

Later in the session, as he was about to leave, Mike paused at the door of the office. Although there remained some hint of a tremor in his voice, there was an unmistakable air of renewed confidence in him. With his head held high, and his posture erect, he turned and said, "Maybe I won't have to kill myself. Maybe all I need to do is learn how to build a door." Even though we had only explored and transformed the metaphor for a few seconds, the metaphor of building a door was to ultimately have far-reaching effects.*

MIKE BEGINS TO OPEN A DOOR IN THE WALL

By the second session Mike had already begun to show significant movement. The day after our first session, Mike attended a gay and lesbian group meeting on a local college campus. Although he sat at the back of the room, cried throughout most of the meeting, and did not actively participate, he decided to continue to attend in hopes of broadening his social contacts in an accepting environment.

The metaphor of the door was not mentioned again in these sessions, yet every week, Mike had trusted enough to "open the door of his wall" just a little wider to let me in, and to let others in as well. During these two meetings, the metaphor of the door was not discussed, but it was lived.

A Dream of "Sara"

Shortly after our third session, Mike was approached by another male member of the gay and lesbian group and asked to go out on a date. Overcoming extreme anxiety about the prospect, Mike agreed and enjoyed the evening spent at a movie and "cruising" a local mall.

---

*By asking Mike "What image comes to mind when you think of the giant wall?," Mike could be helped to further explore his metaphor of the wall *as an image*. The therapist could also ask Mike "What would it be like for you if you did get rid of the wall?"

Mike appears to have accepted the transformation suggested by the therapist that what Mike needed to do is put a door in the wall. Prior to introducing such a change, however, it is usually preferable to ask how the *client* would change the metaphor. For example, the therapist might ask, "What if you could change the image of the giant wall in some way besides pushing it away? How might you change it?"

His greatest fear during and after the date was that he would ultimately be asked to participate in sexually intimate behavior, for which he was not ready. During our session, Mike role-played with me how he would refuse such sexual activity if it was suggested to him.

During this fourth session, Mike also discussed a repetitive dream he has had regularly over the course of several years, in which he saw a female he called "Sara" being stalked by Death. In his dream, there was always a mysterious castle with high fortress-like walls surrounded by a moat in very dark surroundings. Outside of the castle, Death was stalking the figure of Sara. Mike stated that he strongly identified with Sara, and actually thought he loved her. Sara was always seen standing in "the light," a phenomenon Mike could not explain, and she was both armless and unable to be visualized below the waist. He envied her ability to be serene and calm when faced with death. He commented that she was similar to a figure that he had drawn on several previous occasions when he was sad or depressed. After talking at length about Sara and his dream, I asked if he would be willing to bring to a session some of his art work that contained Sara. He agreed.

THE NIGHT CARRIES THE BURDEN OF SADNESS

The fifth meeting began uneventfully. Mike opened the session reporting that on a subsequent date he had been pressured to engage in sexual activity which he had successfully refused, using the techniques we had role-played in the previous session. Furthermore, Mike had "come out" to both of his parents during dinner two nights ago when they began questioning him about his sudden increase in social activities. His "coming out," though quite upsetting, led to a discussion between himself and his parents about the nature of human dignity. After his disclosure, he found it very difficult to sleep and experienced extreme terror during the night. Finally abandoning hope of sleep, he had spent several hours writing a poem which he brought and shared with me during our session. One line in particular stood out as I read his very moving composition.

In that line, he referred to the night as "carrying the burden of sadness." I asked him what that burden was all about, and he said he didn't know. At first, he tried to say that the "sadness" was really frustration, and later he said maybe it was just fatigue. But every time he tried to deny the meaning of sadness, I would remind him that what he had actually written was "sadness," and not "fatigue" or "frustration." As we talked about the "burden of sadness," his eyes began to fill with tears and his face became a deep red. He said he really didn't know exactly what he had meant when he wrote the words, but he guessed that what he had written was in fact reflective of what he experienced every day as darkness approached. With the coming of night, he feels overwhelmed with sadness so great he thinks that it is likely that he will die under the weight of it.

I asked him what the weight came from. He said he didn't know.* I asked him what would happen if he let the weight of sadness go. He said he couldn't let it go because to let it go would be weak. If he let it go, he would cry and he hadn't cried since he was five years old.** By then the tears were almost brimming over, yet he managed to hold them back. He began to choke and cough, and apologized for his coughing. I commented that perhaps he was choked by the sadness. He looked at me and said, with tears beginning to fall softly down his cheeks, "I am so tired, I want to let down the weight; I just don't know how; I just can't do it. The tears you see now are just overflow, but I don't know where they come from, or if I start where they will ever end. The sadness is so deep; I don't know how far down it goes."

As he was very much in touch with his "burden of sadness," I asked him to pause and recall for me an early memory, hoping to reach some of the source of his burden. With tears still brimming over his eyes, he became very quiet and subdued. His breathing slowed spontaneously, his eyes focused on an indeterminate place beyond me, and he thought for quite a few moments. He appeared to be in a mild trance, and he remained in this state for nearly thirty minutes. I did

---

*Questions such as "What is the burden about?" and "Where did the weight come from?" emphasize logical communication and cognition. By asking Mike to describe the *image* that comes to mind when he thinks of the night "carrying the burden of sadness," the therapist could invite Mike to explore the metaphor by using sensory imaginal cognition. After exploring the metaphoric image, Mike could then be invited to transform it. The distinction between logical cognition and imaginal cognition, and their relationship to metaphoric cognition, is discussed in Chapter 5.

**Even though Mike rejects the therapist's "what if" suggestion for transforming the metaphor, the interchange leads to further understanding of Mike's "burden of sadness."

not interrupt once he began speaking, sensing that what he was saying was leading to an important end.

The first memory that he recalled with great pain and emotion was placed by him at the age of two-and-a-half years. He recalled witnessing through the bars of his crib a beating which his father inflicted upon his mother one night, and then remembered that his mother came to hide in the dark beside his crib, whimpering and whispering to him to "be quiet so Daddy won't find me." He then related in rapid succession a series of increasingly horrific memories, all of which took place in the night, and all of which involved him being alone and witness to violence, with no one to protect him or comfort him.

After the third memory was recounted, he paused and then began to cry with shaking sobs, repeating two or three times, "My God! How could I have forgotten!" and "Steven! Steven!" He then shared a final memory, one in which he recounted the "forgotten" death of a "forgotten" brother. Although he had been seven years old at the time, he had "forgotten" both his brother and the events of his sudden death at the age of 18 during a rainy night in which he was killed in an accident. Mike recalled huddling outside his parents' bedroom door, clutching his blanket and listening to his mother emit mournful wailing sobs as his father obtained details of the accident from someone on the phone. He also recalled the drive in the night to the hospital—a drive during which his parents sat in empty silence and no one spoke to him about what had happened. When they arrived at the hospital, Mike was left to wait in the car, with rain falling around him, and though no one ever told him so directly, he knew that his idolized older brother was dead. In the days following Steven's death, Mike recalled holding in all of his grief. He was not allowed to attend the funeral. After the burial, Steven's pictures and possessions were removed from the house. No one ever spoke of Steven again. Mike had successfully avoided consciously remembering the event until now.

After the last memory was finished and his tears had stopped, I asked him for a "snapshot" of the final memory, and finally invited him to transform it.* In the transformation he offered, he said he would have liked to have been allowed to grieve at the time of his brother's death, and to have had someone acknowledge how sad he was. The

---

*It would be desirable to ask Mike to describe the image of the moment in the memory that stands out most vividly, how he felt at that moment, and why he felt that way.

transformed "snapshot" he offered was one of himself grieving.* The session lasted nearly two hours.

Through exploring early memories associated with the metaphor of his "burden of sadness," Mike not only "remembered" a forgotten brother, he uncovered at least some of the sources for his "burden of sadness" and began a grieving process that was more than a decade overdue. As Mike relived the horror of learning about his brother's death and was able to release much of the emotion and sorrow held back for many years, he opened the door of his wall even further. For the first time since he was five, he had allowed himself to cry in the presence of another human being.

I AM SARA

After our previous emotional session, Mike had returned home and that night had dreamed again about "Sara." He brought with him to this sixth session a large canvas on which he had painted the dominant image of his dream. As he presented the painting to me, he commented about his strong identification with the figure, and the feeling that he had while he was painting that "I am Sara." In light of this comment, I felt safe in considering Sara to be a metaphoric representation of Mike's self-image. Our previous session had been very emotionally charged, and since Mike had brought the canvas, spending time talking about his art work seemed a way to be supportive and to slow the pace of therapy a bit. Our discussion of the metaphoric image of Sara provided evidence of continuing change.

M: Well here it is…a painting of Sara, just like I promised.

T: Thank you for bringing it! Tell me about it. (*We then propped the painting on my desk and Mike pulled up his chair so we were both very close to the painting.*)

M: Well, here is Sara, in the bottom left-hand corner. I painted her pretty large, bigger than when I saw her in my dream a few weeks ago. Remember the dream?

---

*Again, it is preferable to ask Mike to describe *his image* of himself grieving, how he felt at that moment, and why he felt that way. It may seem, as in this case, that the answers to the latter two questions are obvious or have already been stated or implied. I have found, however, that asking these questions often yields important additional information about the client's feelings and subjective experience.

T: Yes, of course. Go on.

M: Well anyway, there she is. Doesn't she look serene?

T: The detail is so fine.

M: Do you notice how she is standing in the light. She's al-
        ways in the light. The light seems to radiate out of her.
        That's one thing I don't understand. If she's me or I'm
        her, what is that light? I don't feel like I'm in the light.

T: What if the light was the healthy part of you that keeps
        you going and hopeful even when things look bleak?*

M: If I thought there could be a healthy part of me shining in
        the light and radiating light and peace, it would give me
        hope to go on. Maybe I could accept myself as...

T: ...as gay?

M: As gay... that's the part I have an impossible time with. I
        can't even say it without stumbling over the words.

T: I notice she is only drawn from the waist up.

M: Yes. That's all of her I can see. I tried to paint lower, but
        the colors didn't work. But the top of her is beautiful, so
        I just painted that part. She also doesn't have any arms. I
        didn't give her arms.

T: I get the feeling that she would feel weak and vulnerable with-
        out arms. What's your feeling about her not having arms?

M: Actually, from the back I guess her shape would look
        like a tombstone...You're right though, definitely weak
        and defenseless. I hadn't thought of that.

T: Almost dead without those arms.

M: Maybe, but not quite. You see? Behind her. In the dreams
        there was the skull of Death stalking her, but in this pic-
        ture, there is no Death. It is still very dark, but Death
        isn't around any more. Maybe he is hiding somewhere
        behind a tree or something, but he's not close anymore.
        And in my dream there was a castle in the distance, but
        there is no castle here either. It still looks mystical and
        very dark, but no more Death. And no castle.

T: What do you suppose happened to Death and the castle?

M: I don't know. I just didn't feel like painting them any
        more. I paint what I feel and they weren't part of what I
        felt. They're just gone; I don't know where.

---

*The therapist introduces an encouraging interpretation of the light as the healthy part of
Mike. My preference would have been to invite Mike to explore the image of the light before
making this suggestion.

T: How would you change the image of Sara if you could?

M: She would develop arms.

T: What do you suppose it would take for Sara to develop arms? (*Silence for at least a full minute*)

M: She would have to be free. (*Silence for 60 seconds as we gaze at the painting together*) As I think about it, I think maybe she has arms growing, but we just can't see them yet—embryonic arms.

T: There's an interesting idea! How will the arms grow?

M: I'm not sure how that works. I think it's important to stay in the light. I don't know exactly, but light helps things grow.

T: I'm interested to know—If you could change this painting in any way, how would you change it?

M: Hmmm. Good question. (*Silence*) If I could change it I would paint her whole. She would have a whole body, and all of her would be in the light.

T: And if you could take a snapshot of just a part of that new painting, what would the snapshot look like?

M: It would be of Sara. She would have a whole body and...she would be dancing.

T: When you say she would be dancing, I get an image of her spinning like a ballerina, up on one toe, with her skirts swirling around her.

M: It's funny you should say that. It's just what I was thinking. Spinning like a ballerina, with her arms outstretched...she would have arms. She would be graceful, and swirling. She would be free.*

T: That would be good. Thank you for sharing her with me. It will be interesting to see how Sara develops.

M: You're right. And to watch her arms grow.

In the two sessions that followed the metaphorical work with the painting of Sara and the discussion of her potential for growth and development, Mike continued to explore and integrate the material we had previously discussed. In this time period he broke off his relationship with his boyfriend when the pressure for sexual intimacy

---

*The therapist shared her image with Mike and it resonated with Mike's own image. While this intervention was successful, the suggested procedure is for the therapist to ask Mike to explore *his* image of Sara dancing, after which the therapist could share her own image if needed.

became too intense, but quickly found another male companion who was respectful of Mike's needs and was willing to offer Mike some emotional "breathing room." Finding a companion who would not immediately pressure him to engage in sexual activity gave Mike an opportunity to come to a greater acceptance of himself as gay and acceptance of himself as a sexual being, before he was faced with the vulnerability which would come with sexual intimacy. With this new companion, Mike was able to gain further mastery over his panic and agoraphobia, and was able to hike into the local mountains and go on a weekend camping trip. Although anxious to an extent bordering on panic, he was able to effectively use the cognitive strategies we had practiced in our sessions to control his anxiety.

THE LITTLE BOY LOCKED UP IN THE CASTLE IS ME!

In the ninth session, Mike introduced several new metaphors which led to another moving early memory. At one point during the session, Mike commented that he felt like the fable character Chicken Little, who always feared the sky was falling. It led to the following exchange:

M: I feel like I have always had to hold up my own sky. I can never let go or it will all come crashing down. Even as a young child, I was holding up that sky...but it didn't seem so heavy then.

T: You couldn't feel secure if you thought the sky would collapse if you let go.

M: Things almost did collapse once.

T: Really? Tell me about it. (*At this point both of us shifted in our chairs, sort of "settling in" for the telling of a story. Then everything became quiet and Mike became very calm and peaceful. The only sound was that of the air conditioner humming.*)

M: I have this memory that just came to me. I was five or six years old. My mother thought my dad was having an affair. She decided this day to confirm it. She put me and my little brother into the car and drove to this woman's house. Sure enough his car was parked out front. My mom parked behind his car and broke down sobbing. Then she started to throw up. I was afraid she was going to take me and my brother into that apartment to confront him. I didn't want to do that. She threw up and threw up. I didn't know somebody could throw up so much. I just sat there frozen. It was kind of unreal. I didn't know what to do. I felt out of it. I was really afraid of what would happen to me and my brother if she left my father. I knew I was adopted and I wondered if they would send me back. It was really clear to me then that I wasn't part of their family and didn't belong *(begins to get teary-eyed, but does not cry now)*. Then she wrote him a note saying that she knew. She told me to go and put it on his car, under the windshield wiper. I remember that I hated that. I was afraid he would see me, but I did it. Then we left and drove home.

T: If you could take a snapshot of that memory, what would it look like?

M: It would be me walking up to the car to put the note there like she said. While I was walking, I vowed that I would never grow up. I would die first.*

T: If you could change the memory in any way, how would you change it?

M: I would have died then. It wasn't scary to me then. After that experience, I was still really a little boy, but I thought like an old man. I still do.

T: What happened to the little boy?

M: He went away. Part of him did die, I think.

T: He died?

M: Maybe not dead, but he might as well have been dead. I guess he just got sealed off.

T: When you say "sealed off," I get an image of the castle you described in your dream. You said you didn't know what it meant or who lived there. I wonder if he got sealed off there—in the castle.

M: Behind thick walls.

T: And maybe outside the castle...

M: Death was stalking. The little boy said he'd rather die than grow up. Maybe death was always out there waiting. It makes sense.

---

*Following the interview protocol, the therapist could ask Mike how he felt at that moment and why he felt that way.

T: What did the little boy do behind the castle walls all these years?

M: I guess he sat in the dark and was very quiet.

T: Until now.

M: Until now.

T: Where is the little boy now?

M: In. . . . .the. . . . . .castle. . . . . .OH, GOD!!

T: What?

M: I'M THE CASTLE!!!!! The little boy is locked up in ME! God, I didn't know! (*Gets teary but doesn't really cry*)

T: What is the little boy doing in the castle now?

M: Lately, he has been creating so much mischief. Why would he do that? It has caused me so much pain!

T: What do you suppose would make the little boy act out and create mischief?

M: I don't know.

T: Think about it for a minute. Why does any little boy create mischief?

M: He wants to be seen...He wants to be *heard*. (*His eyes fill with tears, his face becomes red, and he becomes very still.*) (*Silence... [He is fighting tears.]*)

T: What if you let the little boy out for just a few minutes.

M: (*Silent. Tears begin to fall*)

T: Could you do that? Just for a minute?

M: Nods. Tears falling.

T: Imagine him sitting here with us, maybe in that chair. You can talk to him.

M: I don't know where to begin. (*Crying*)

T: You have so many feelings.

M: So does he.

T: What does he want to say?

M: He just wants to cry. (*Cries for several minutes*)

T: (Softly) What makes him cry?

M: His innocence is gone. She took it away.

T: She?

M: His mother. She stole his innocence and it will never come back. The innocence is lost. (*Crying*) He was young and fun and full of smiles. He was happy and she took it away.

T: How did she take it away?

M: He doesn't remember. Maybe just pulling him into her troubles–making him her little man. He didn't want to be her little man.

T: What else does the little boy say?

M: He wants to come out of the castle but he doesn't know who he is anymore. He wants to come out and be a little boy and be loved. But he's scared, and he doesn't know how to get out. And I don't know how to help him...I'm afraid to let him out.

T: It's scary to think of letting him out.

M: Yes. I wouldn't know what to do.

T: What if there was a real little boy here with us and he was scared, and looking to you for help, what would you do?*

M: I would pick him up and hold him. I would embrace him (*Tears spill*) (*Silence for a few moments*) That's it, isn't it? I have to love the little boy so he can come out and grow up? How do I let him grow up? How do I get him to catch up to my body? Do I have to do something special?

T: What if you find a way to let him out of the castle so he can be in the light? In the light he would grow.

M: But I'm afraid of all the mischief he could cause if he just came out all of a sudden.**

T: What if for right now you didn't let him all the way out. What if you just left the castle doors unlocked.

M: Then maybe he could find his own way out. Slowly.

T: That might be easier for you.

M: I think so. Will I know when he's out?

T: I think you'll know.

In this session, through the exploration of the metaphor of Chicken Little and Mike's feeling that he has had to hold up his own sky, an

---

*This intervention is similar to Lawrence LeShan's (1977) "time machine" approach. LeShan asks the client to imagine that, as the adult person he or she is now, the client could travel back in time to the moment being recalled in the early memory. What would the client do with and say to the child in the memory?

**This illustrates how our clients may help us when we invite a metaphoric "what if" transformation that is too scary. The castle walls serve a protective as well as a restrictive function. Mike reminded the therapist of the scary consequences that would follow if the boy was let out all of a sudden. This allowed the therapist to realign with Mike and to invite Mike to begin by taking a small step toward growth and change.

early memory was spontaneously recalled. As we moved from one metaphor to another, exploring/transforming each in turn, many links were formed and a clearer picture of Mike's basic issues emerged. Although all of his problems were not clearly illuminated in this session, the introduction of the metaphor of the little boy was especially helpful. Through a discussion of the little boy who lived in the castle, Mike was able to bring out painful emotional material that he was unable to talk about more directly. Also, through the exploration of the metaphor and the invitation to talk to the "little boy" within himself, he was able to begin to focus on feelings of lost innocence. By suggesting that Mike leave the castle doors unlocked so that the "little boy" could slowly and more safely emerge, the therapist made progress seem less threatening.

A KNOT IN THE STOMACH–I WANT TO GIVE BIRTH

The surprising revelations of the 10th session were introduced through another exercise of the creative imagination that took the form of an essay which Mike had composed the night before our session. Once again, following a familiar pattern, Mike had been overcome with sadness and a sense of impending death with the coming of nightfall. In an earlier session, it had been suggested that he write down his feelings when they started to overpower him, and although he was not confident that this would help, he decided to try, directing the essay to the therapist. Since he felt sure that he would not survive to see our session, he had started to write the essay as a "kind of last will and testament." In the composition, which he wrote through tears, he described feeling a coldness in his stomach and a knot of fear also located there–both of which he associated with impending death. He wrote, "My life is over, of this I have no doubt. I am so hopelessly alone, I cry and no one hears me. Life *will* end now." However, he said that as he wrote, he began to think that the feelings he was experiencing in the present were the feelings of the little boy stuck in the castle.

As I write this my thoughts go out to him, and I wonder if I could ask him what he fears. I think he feels desperately alone. Is this a coincidence that what he feels, I feel? I think not. I need to remember that the key is not to shut him in but to embrace him.

He stated that as soon as he had written these words he felt a sense of serenity and peace replace the panic and doom that he felt only minutes earlier. He then began to question what, beyond darkness, had brought about the fear.

In our session, I asked him to describe other situations in which he was aware of feeling the coldness and the knot of fear which he thinks signals death. He responded that any time he "lets go" he has the same feeling. He remembers that as a young teenager the only way he could "let go" was to get drunk, dress in women's clothes, and pretend to be someone else. As an adult, the only time he ever really "let go" was during sexual contact, but sexual release was also followed by the same coldness and knot in the stomach, and by the feeling that because he has "let go" he will die.* The following then transpired between us:

T: I notice you described the sensation of sexual release the same way you described the fear in the little boy last night. In both cases, you fear dying. I wonder if those two feelings could be associated.

M: I never noticed that. But it is the same sick, cold, empty feeling. Exactly the same...Exactly.

T: How early in your life can you remember having that feeling?

M: So long ago. I don't recall. Probably whenever the little boy was submerged and went under...under cover.

T: When do you suppose that was?

M: Before I was 10 or 11. By then I already couldn't have any fun. I couldn't let go even then. I was already locked up.

T: Any early memories come to mind?

M: No. (*Pause*) I did kind of have that cold, sick feeling today, though.

T: The same feeling?

---

*Mike could be invited to explore and transform the metaphoric images of "letting go," "coldness," and the "knot in the stomach."

M: Just a feeling. Not even a whole memory.

T: A piece of a memory?

M: (*Nods*)

T: Can you describe it for me?

M: It's not very complete. Just a flash.

T: That's O.K. Describe what you can remember.

M: O.K. Well, this morning while I was eating my cereal at the breakfast bar, I got the cold, sick feeling, and it bothered me, so I stopped eating. Then I left for school. I thought I'd tell you about it. It wasn't even a real memory. Just a fuzzy sort of a fragment of a memory. Like a peek into the past. And then it was gone.

T: What happened to make you feel sick, do you know?

M: This is going to sound silly. The red lobster that sits on our kitchen counter. It's been there for years. It never bothered me before. You know, a plastic-type kitchen decoration? It's been there years. I never even pay attention to it. But today it was in my way and when I picked it up to move it, that's when I got the sick feeling.

T: You noticed the lobster and felt sick.

M: Yeah. I said this was going to sound ridiculous. I tried to put the paper over it, but I knew it was there, and then I had this flash–like a fuzzy piece of memory for just a second, way off in the corner of my mind. And then, before I could really look at it, it was gone. Then I didn't want any more breakfast, so I left.

T: What was the memory?

M: Not a whole memory.

T: The fuzzy flash.

M: I wouldn't tell this to anybody but you. Anybody else would think I was crazy to get upset about this. I saw the lobster in the tub. That's it. I can't figure out why that would get me feeling sick. Maybe you can figure it out.

T: Well, let's see. You saw the lobster in the tub?

M: Yes, in "Bill's" tub.

T: In "Bill's" tub?

M: Well it's his tub now, but at the time it was just the family tub. It was way before we remodeled and before "Bill"

was born. I think I must have been just about three or
four.

T: So you remember the lobster in the tub. Anything else?

M: Well, as I sit here talking about it, some things do sort of
come back, but it's not very complete.

T: That's O.K.

M: I seem to recall that there was a party going on in the
house. A fancy party. Maybe they were even serving
lobster.

T: Mmm hmm.

M: I'm remembering more of this. I was in the bathroom. I
was going to take a bath, but first I was standing near the
toilet to go to the bathroom. I don't remember much.
It's fuzzy. I'm trying...That's all. It seems like there was
more but I can't remember now. (*Pause*) That's it. I really
wish I could remember the rest, but I can't right now.

T: Maybe that's all there is to remember for now. Maybe
you'll remember more later.

M: (*Brief pause*) Well, as I sit here now, I do remember the
tub full of water and the lobster floating on top of the
water. Maybe I was going to take a bath before the party.

T: You were pretty young. Did you do your bath yourself?

M: No, my parents would supervise. (*Suddenly bending over
and rubbing his stomach/lower abdomen, and emitting a soft
moan*) Ugh!

T: Are you O.K.? You look like you're in pain.

M: I don't know what just happened. Just talking about this,
the adrenaline is starting now. Just like last night. And
my stomach is in a knot (*Rubbing stomach*). My heart is
pounding. I feel like I'm going to die! I can hear my
heart pounding. (*His face is ashen and he begins to perspire.*)

T: You're not going to die, Mike, but it sounds like you're
frightened. Just like last night. Just like every night. Just
take a deep breath. Don't talk for a while. Your heart
will slow down. You're O.K. We'll just sit here breathing slowly until you're better. We have lots of time. Just
take a deep breath and blow it out. That's good. Slow it
down. That's it.

M: (*Breathing slower*) I hate this panic feeling. I'm cold in-
        side—dry ice freezing a hole through my core. It's the
        door. The memory. It's locked. I can't get out.

T: You can't get out.

M: Someone is there with me. (*Rubbing his stomach*) Oh, the
        knot! It's fuzzy. I'm trying but I can't see who it is. The
        whole picture is fuzzy. Like very bad still shots. All out
        of focus. Someone is there with me. I'm naked for my
        bath. They are standing over me. I'm cold. I'm going to
        die. I can hear my heart. I don't know who it is. My
        heart is racing. The little boy wants to cry. He wants to
        be let out. (*Eyes fill with tears; face is flushed bright red; wring-
        ing his hands*)

T: Let him cry, Mike. He needs to cry.

M: (*Cries for several minutes, softly*) (*Rubbing his stomach*) The
        knot is gone; the cold is gone. (*Whispering*) I was mo-
        lested, wasn't I? This morning at breakfast, I couldn't see
        the memory, but I had this idea. I thought, "This is it. I
        was molested." I didn't see the whole memory—just a
        shadow. But I knew. I felt it. Somebody did it to me.

T: Sounds like it.

M: But I can't remember who. Or what they did.

T: You don't have to remember now.

M: Not today.

T: You just remember how scary it felt.

M: Cold. Like I was going to die. Just like I feel every night.
        (*Pause*) Did it just happen once?

T: I don't know. (*Handing him another box of tissue*)

M: (*Composing himself*) I want to let him out. Do you re-
        member when I told you I wanted to be a woman be-
        cause I wanted to give birth? Well, I want to give birth to
        the little boy. How do I start the gestation?

T: I think the gestation has been there a long time already.
        The little boy has been gestating for years.

M: (*Smiling*) Like an elephant.

T: A long and very heavy gestation. (*Heavy like the sky; heavy
        like the "burden of the night" in his poetry*)

M: How does he get born though?

T: Through labor. What you're doing now is labor. Painful
        and long, but in the end the child is born.

M: How long is labor?

T: In people, it varies a lot. But what about elephants? The gestation is long, maybe the labor is long too.

M: This won't be done tomorrow.

T: Probably not, but you've come a distance already.

M: I want it over. I want to give birth already.

T: What will it be like to have him born?

M: A relief. And scary.

T: In what way?

M: Newborns make a lot of noise when they cry. You don't know what to expect. It could make a person panic.

T: When you say that, I get an image. I see a boy standing on one side of a wood fence that he can't see through. There is a dog barking loudly on the other side—a big deep bark. Just then another boy, who owns the dog, comes outside and goes to swing the gate open. And in that one moment before the gate swings wide to let out the barking dog, the little boy stands there frozen in panic expecting some fierce, vicious animal to lunge out. Have you ever had an experience like that?

M: Yes, when I was younger.

T: What if when the dog rushes out it turns out to be some little bit of a thing with a big bark?

M: Like a dachshund...

T: A dachshund who runs up...

M: And licks the boy all over. (*Smiles*) Pretty harmless.

T: Pretty harmless.

M: What you're saying is that if I let the little boy out—even if he cries—letting him out won't necessarily be as bad as I think.

T: Maybe not.

M: Maybe not.

T: Maybe he's already peeking out.

M: I think so. Do you think I'll ever be able to open the door and let him all the way out?

T: I believe you will. (*End of session*)

The process of talking to the little boy, or being in contact with his feelings, which was suggested in the prior session, was used by Mike at home to deal with his bedtime fears of death. At a time when he was certain he would die, by making a metaphoric shift and methodically exploring his feelings as the feelings of a little boy, Mike was able to control his panic and achieve a sense of peace and calm which allowed him to sleep. Through the creative process of writing, Mike began to understand his feelings, correctly identifying his somatic sensations and recognizing them as signs of fear and not true harbingers of death.

Having worked with early memories in the past, Mike was more comfortable with the recollection process in this session, and, with patience and encouragement, was able to allow his memory of molestation to surface. After the memory of the molestation incident was relatively complete, rather than immediately ask for a transformation, I decided to proceed gently and allow Mike to compose himself. Although I never had the opportunity to ask him for a transformation of the memory, he spontaneously offered one, stating that he wanted to let the little boy out. Interestingly, the process which he suggested, (*"giving birth"*) was itself metaphorical.

Given that the concerns Mike identified as the most important focus for his therapy were his problems with sexual identity, it was significant that he framed his desire to "let the little boy out" as the process of giving birth. In his earlier paintings and dreams of Sara, Mike had been unable to visualize her generative body parts ("the colors didn't work"). In talking about "giving birth" to the "little boy" feelings and emotions which had been locked behind the metaphorical castle walls, Mike was now speaking in active terms (though metaphorically) about successfully giving birth. It seemed that his metaphoric construction of self as a generative self was now operative and functioning. In a dramatic shift in his metaphoric structure of reality, he now appeared to view himself as symbolically able to bring forth new life. His generative processes were capable of working. Although he feared the metaphorical process of labor, and was unsure of what to do with a metaphoric baby who cries, he was on the right developmental track, for those are fears common to anyone facing labor.

The use of metaphors of light and dark were also enduring and meaningful. Mike characterized the "little boy" as having been in the dark sitting quiet and still for years.* Making reference again to the

---

*The metaphoric image of the little boy sitting quiet and still in the dark and Mike's metaphor of the night carrying the burden of sadness symbolize both Mike's emotional pain and an attempt to protect himself from that pain. This is poignantly depicted in two of Mike's early memories, recalled in association with his exploring the BURDEN OF SADNESS metaphor: (1) the memory image of his mother hiding in the dark beside his crib, whispering to him to "be quiet so Daddy won't find me," and (2) the subsequent recall of "the drive in the night" to the hospital during which his parents "sat in empty silence" and no one spoke to him about the sudden death of his brother Steven.

phenomenon of the light, he was seeking to let the little boy out into the light so he could grow. Letting his long hidden emotions and feelings out would ultimately allow Mike to move into mature adulthood. Years ago, Mike vowed that he would never grow up. Much of his emotional development seemed to have been arrested at this early stage of life. Yet his body had continued to grow and Mike now found himself in adult situations (especially sexual situations) with which he was emotionally ill equipped to cope. By finally bringing the "little boy" feelings into awareness, Mike would be able to become a more fully developed human being.

It was also interesting to note the recurrent theme of "coming out." With regard to his homosexuality, much of our very early work related to the process of "coming out" to his family and to the gay and lesbian community. More recently, the issue was the "coming out" of the little boy in his metaphor and coming out of the locked bathroom in his early memory. Implicit in the notion of "coming out" was the idea that one was coming out of darkness and moving into the light and awareness. Thus, both between and within metaphors there was a symbolic consistency in Mike's metaphoric structure of reality (discussed in the next chapter).

In working with the metaphors, I attempted to suggest a transformation process that would be gentle and relatively slow. I suggested that Mike leave the door of the castle unlocked, but not open wide, so that the little boy could come out slowly; and at the end of the 10th session, I suggested that perhaps the little boy was already peeking out.

One of Mike's historical problems had been an inability to tolerate bathing with his clothing removed, and difficulty looking at himself in the mirror. In light of the memory of the probable bathroom molestation incident, an explanation for Mike's behavior is suggested. Keeping his clothing on in the present may have evolved from his vulnerability when he was naked as a child preparing for his bath. The metaphors he used to describe the "little boy" were consistent with the bath memory that eventually was related during the session. He said that he believed the feelings of the cold and the knot in his stomach first began "at a time when the little boy was submerged or went under."

THE PAINS OF LABOR

Mike returned for his 11th session experiencing intense emotional pain from a week-long series of flashbacks of early memory images related to abuse incidents in his childhood. In this session we explored his fear as the walls that surrounded the little boy (feelings) began to crumble. He was beginning to hear the metaphorical baby cry, and it was frightening for him. He said he felt very much like the little child that went into submerged hiding at the age of five, and he felt a need to be consoled and protected. While he was reminded of the inner strength which helped him survive to adulthood, we agreed to meet more frequently until this crisis passed.

In concrete terms he was given specific strategies to use to cope with his flood of emotion ("tips on how to care for a metaphorical crying baby"). Although this was a time of great emotional pain and upheaval, Mike was progressing toward his goals. The pains of labor were at their peak as he struggled to give birth to the emotions of the child within. It was clear that the transformations which first took place symbolically in Mike's creative imagination during our sessions were becoming visible in his life.

COMING INTO THE LIGHT

Mike had arrived at a particularly painful and vulnerable point in his therapy when he would confront the reality of his abuse and the violence he had witnessed in his life. His commitment to therapy, already great, took on a new urgency. He wanted very much to "give birth" to a new and more integrated self. During months of therapy we talked, and the seasons changed outside the office window. Mike commented once on how the seasons (metaphorically) matched his progress, with wind and rain punctuating some of his saddest memories, and spring blossoming as he began to move more quickly ahead. He often used the metaphor of coming into the light; for him it seemed to have the greatest meaning.

During winter and spring, Mike made many positive changes in his life. His memories of molestation became clearer and he eventually confronted his father with his recollections of incest and moved out of the family home. The sheets which once covered his mirrors came down, and he was able to bathe without discomfort. His painting and creative writing were brought out of seclusion and shared with others. He made the decision to return to school, enrolling in classes at a local college, and joined the staff of a school literary magazine. He became active in the college gay and lesbian student group and found satisfaction in political activities that supported gay rights. He volunteered at a crisis "hot line." He made good friends.

Over time, he ventured farther and farther away from home, initially with intense anxiety, but later with only mild apprehension. His panic attacks stopped. He slept at night most of the time, and he no longer dreamed about castles and moats and death stalking. Yet he remained fragile, and his emotional equilibrium was easily shattered. Every movement forward was well planned and methodically executed. There were tears and setbacks. There were days of despair. There were extra sessions to ease him over crisis periods. Eventually, he developed patience with his own progress, and became more confident of the stability and permanence of the changes he was making in his life.

THE LITTLE BOY CONTINUES TO GROW

Termination was necessitated by my impending departure from the counseling center, and it proved to be a difficult process. Although Mike did not yet feel emotionally ready to be on his own, the situation of forced termination provided an opportunity for his development in new directions. Spurred by the knowledge that our time together was coming to an end, Mike surged ahead, making forays further and further outside of his ever-expanding comfort zone, and building new relationships and developing closer friendship ties with his peers.

One day, Mike began our session with the startling announcement that he had decided to pursue his education in another part of the country. He had begun to investigate universities out of state and was planning to move. Although the thought of going far away caused him some anxiety, he stated that his increasing ability to travel locally without panic had convinced him that he could go wherever he wanted. He was confident of his ability to succeed. Eventually, he was accepted at a university, and many of our later sessions were devoted to discussing his hopes and anxieties.

As the termination process drew to a close, Mike reflected on his experience of therapy. Looking back on our time together, he identified the use of his creative expression through writing and painting as the most significant aspects of his therapy. He expressed the belief that through the use of his creative expression he was able to explore the most painful parts of himself and gain an understanding that was meaningful to him. Although the final session was emotional, it was clear that Mike had prepared himself to execute his plans, and his intention was to resume therapy at the college counseling center of his new school.

EPILOGUE: "MOSTLY, NOW, MY LIFE IS IN THE LIGHT"

Several years following the termination of therapy, Mike contacted me. The young man who presented himself in the lobby of my office on a summer afternoon was a striking contrast to the person that I greeted in the lobby of the counseling center years before. Mike, as he stood to greet me now, was flush with health and vigor. His face no longer was pale and gaunt, but tanned and full. He appeared sturdy and strong. The tremble in his hand was gone, replaced by a firm handshake. His lips were no longer cracked, dry and quivering; rather they curved upward in a warm engaging smile.

In the hour that followed, Mike brought me up to date on his progress and his plans. He had completed his baccalaureate degree and in the fall would be moving again, this time to a university in still another part of the country, where he would begin graduate studies. He found moving to be an adventure, and looked forward to a future that he anticipated would be filled with promise. Although he occasionally was confronted with a new memory from his past, or depressed by a sudden flashback to the violence of his childhood, Mike reported that he had been able to weather those periods of stress with the help and support of his friends. In talking of his experiences, he returned to the metaphor of the light, saying, "At those times when the path becomes very dark, I don't get so afraid anymore. I have traveled those paths before, with you, and I know with great confidence that the light is there, just around the corner. Mostly, now, my life is in the light."

It was clear from this final meeting that through the metaphorical process of gestating and giving birth which had begun years before, Mike was reaching maturity. Mike had created a door in his emotional fortress and had found the courage to open it. The little boy had come out into the light, and he had grown into his manhood.

5

I Think, Therefore I Am a Tea Kettle: Metaphor Therapy and the Metaphoric Structure of Reality

We can best understand the function and therapeutic value of metaphor by appreciating the nature of metaphor in general. Most of us are aware of metaphor's role in everyday speech. We may not realize that our abstract concepts depend on metaphor, that metaphor is vital to the development and evolution of language, and that even our construction of reality is grounded in metaphor. This chapter explores the nature of metaphor and will help clarify how the methods outlined in Part I for working with client-generated metaphors can bring about profound and sometimes rapid change.

The word metaphor is derived from the Greek *meta,* meaning "above or over," and *phorein,* meaning "to carry or bear from one place to another." *Metaphor carries meaning over from one domain to another.* When Romeo declares, "Juliet is the sun," for example, the sun's qualities convey the meaning that is "carried over" to Juliet. Linguists refer to Juliet as the *topic* in this metaphor, and the sun as the *vehicle*–a fitting term (metaphor)–for that aspect of metaphor that "carries or bears" meaning from one thing or domain to another (Winner, 1988).

There appears to be a paradox, however. How can two things be both the same and different at the same time? And how can a statement that is literally false (Juliet is *not* the sun) also be true?

DOES METAPHOR MAKE SENSE OR NONSENSE: TWO PHILOSOPHICAL TRADITIONS

Aristotle held that to "metaphorize" well is a sign of genius in the poet and, in poetry "the greatest thing by far is to be the master of metaphor" (quoted in Ricoeur, 1984, p. 23). In Aristotle's view, metaphor involves giving a thing a name that belongs to something else. Ricoeur (1979) points out that, according to Aristotle, making good metaphors requires the capacity to contemplate similarities. Moreover, good metaphors are vivid because they can "set before the eyes" the sense that they display. It is through this "picturing function" that metaphoric meaning is conveyed (Ricoeur, 1979).

From this view, metaphors make "sense" by pointing to the resemblance between a referent topic (Juliet) and a sensory image (the warmth and radiance of the sun).

In contrast, philosophers following a positivist tradition that emphasizes objectivity, fact, and logic have maintained that metaphors are frivolous and inessential, if not dangerous and logically perverse. From the perspective of positivism, metaphors do not contain or transmit knowledge, have no direct connection with facts, and convey no genuine meaning (Cohen, 1979). Cohen traces this position back to Hobbes and John Locke. In the following Herculean sentence, for example, Locke launches a verbal barrage at figurative language (including metaphor), leaving little doubt about his disdain for such rhetoric:

> If we would speak of things as they are, we must allow that all the art of rhetoric, besides order and clearness, all the artificial and figurative application of words eloquence hath invented, are for nothing else but to insinuate wrong ideas, move the passions, and thereby mislead the judgment, and so indeed are perfect cheats, and therefore, however laudable or allowable oratory may render them in harangues and popular addresses, they are certainly, in all discourses that pretend to inform or instruct, wholly to be avoided; and where truth and knowledge are concerned, cannot but be thought a great fault, either of the language or person that makes use of them. (quoted in Cohen, 1979, p. 2)

Since metaphors are untrue as *literal* statements, we can see why metaphor is viewed as frivolous and inessential by those for whom reality and truth are restricted to the domain of literal meaning and logical thought. In the "either-or" domain of linear logic, sameness and difference are incompatible. Metaphor must be rejected as illogical and untrue.

METAPHORIC LANGUAGE: THE SOURCE OF NOVELTY AND CHANGE IN LANGUAGE AND PSYCHOTHERAPY

The positivist perspective has been challenged by recent developments in a variety of disciplines, including linguistics, philosophy, and cognitive psychology. Winner (1988) suggests that it wasn't until the 1970's that psycholinguists and cognitive psychologists became interested in metaphors because of their realization that metaphor was not a unique, atypical form of language found primarily in poetry. "Instead, metaphor was recognized as a pervasive aspect of ordinary language and as the primary vehicle for language change" (Winner, 1988, p. 16). Metaphors came to be appreciated as the root of the creativity and openness of language, and, thus, as an essential aspect of cognition (Winner, 1988).

In her landmark book, *Philosophy in a New Key* (1942/1979), Langer presents a persuasive argument for the central role of metaphor in the evolution of language and symbolic thought in homo sapiens. Drawing on the work of Philip Wegener, published in 1885, Langer suggests that *metaphor is the principle through which literal language develops* and that our literal language is the repository of "faded metaphors" (p. 140).

Where a precise word is lacking, a speaker resorts to the powers of *logical analogy* (i.e., metaphor) to designate novelty by using a word denoting something else that is a symbol for the thing the speaker means (Langer, 1942/1979). Langer emphasizes the key role of metaphor in the evolution of language and the construction of symbolic meaning. The therapy cases presented in Part I suggest that an analogous process may occur in therapy, i.e., the exploration and transformation of client metaphors can also yield new meanings.

Langer also notes that new expressions and ideas evoke metaphoric expressions. The cases presented in Part I suggest that the inverse can also be true regarding therapeutic change, i.e., new experiences and ideas can result from evoking and transforming metaphoric images. Thus, *just as metaphor is the source of novelty and change in language, exploring and transforming a person's metaphoric imagery can be a source of novelty and change in psychotherapy.*

METAPHORIC COGNITION: A SYNTHESIS OF LOGICAL AND IMAGINAL COGNITION

Part of what makes metaphors a powerful vehicle for therapeutic work is that they combine two modes of cognition—logical and imaginal—into a distinct third form: metaphoric cognition.

We have seen that linguistic metaphors are typically *word-pictures* that create a resemblance between an image and a referent situation. *The metaphor-maker paints a picture with words, combining, and, in fact, integrating non-linear/imaginal communication with linear/verbal communication.* Langer's concept of logical analogy describes that quality of metaphor that integrates the logic of words and the "analogic" of imagery. Lackoff and Johnson (1980) echo Langer's view, maintaining that metaphor is imaginative rationality uniting reason and imagination. Clearly, the concepts of "logical analogy" and "imaginative rationality" describe similar processes that are consistent with the concept of metaphoric cognition as a combination of imaginal and logical cognition.

Logical cognition (referred to in the research literature as propositional/syllogistic cognition) proceeds logically from premise to conclusion. Perhaps the best known example of this form of thought is "Socrates' syllogism":

> Men die.
> Socrates is a man.
> Socrates will die.

The premise, "men die," followed by classifying Socrates as a member of the class called "men," leads inexorably to the logical conclusion that Socrates will die.

Probably due to the influence of logical-positivist philosophy mentioned earlier, only recently has cognitive science launched a program of research to ask whether imagery is another form of, and/or subordinate to, propositional/syllogistic cognition, or whether imagery is a form of cognition in its own right existing independent of propositional cognition, with its own set of rules, principles, and characteristics.

Kosslyn (1980), presents a comprehensive review of research and theory on imagery. He concludes that both *propositional and quasi-pictorial imagery representations are present in memory. The key distinction between the two rests on the difference between* description, *which characterizes propositions, and* depiction, *which is achieved with pictorial representation.* For example, the phrase "the ball is on the box" is a propositional statement that *describes* the relationship between the ball and the box, whereas drawing a picture of a ball resting on a box would be a pictorial representation that *depicts* the relationship between the ball and the box.

As we have seen, metaphors combine both image and word. The metaphoric imagery employed by the metaphor-maker suggests the presence of *imaginal cognitive* processes in the construction of the "word-picture" metaphor, while the fact that the metaphor is expressed in words embedded in the flow of verbal discourse suggests the presence of *propositional/syllogistic cognition.* We can infer that *a third, distinct type of cognition—metaphoric cognition—is involved in the creation of metaphors.* Indeed, *metaphoric cognition appears to integrate both imaginal and propositional/syllogistic cognition.*

METAPHOR: GESTURE EXPRESSED IN WORDS

Based on his exhaustive analysis of videotaped gestures made by subjects while describing a cartoon they had seen (a research project extending over almost a decade), McNeill (1992) observed that gesture reveals a new dimension of the mind that has lain hidden—the imagery of language. He concluded that speech and gesture are elements of a single integrated process; "a synthesis of opposite modes of thought—global-synthetic and instantaneous imagery with linear-segmented temporally extended verbalization" (p. 35).

McNeill's research demonstrates that the nonverbal, imagistic dimension of language is communicated through gestures, while the linear, sequential dimension of language is communicated through words. Thus, gesture, while part of a single integrated linguistic process, remains nonverbal and independent from the verbal aspects of speech.

Metaphor appears to be a special case within linguistic processes, however. As with the verbal-gestural operation discussed by McNeill, metaphor is an integral whole constructed with both imagistic and linear-segmented aspects. The difference is that, in the case of metaphor, the vehicle for expressing the global-synthetic and instantaneous imagistic mode of thought is metaphoric imagery. Thus, *metaphor is gesture expressed in words.*

THE CREATIVE IMAGINATION IN SCIENCE AND PSYCHOTHERAPY

Arthur Miller's fascinating book, *Imagery in Scientific Thought: Creating 20th-Century Physics* (1986), argues persuasively that recent research on imaginal cognition, as well as reflections of creative physicists, supports the view that imaginal cognition is essential to the creation of new ways of looking at things. He reviews the introspections of Albert Einstein and Henri Poincaré, as well as the recollections of Niels Bohr and Werner Heisenberg. These scientists emphasized the central role of mental imagery in contrast to purely syllogistic or verbal modes of thinking in their creative scientific work. Miller asserts that, "Their testimonies against productive [creative] thinking in modes that are purely syllogistic or verbal is reasonable because thinking in these modes can proceed only linearly or stepwise" (p. 223).

I noted earlier that linguistic metaphors are word-pictures generated by metaphoric cognition—a synthesis of imaginal and logical cognition. The metaphor-maker draws out of his or her creative imagination an image that resembles a pattern of meaning present in a specific situation to which the metaphoric image refers (e.g., "I'm just spinning my wheels at this job."). If Miller and the physicists are right in suggesting that imaginal cognition plays a key role in the creation of new ideas, then it seems reasonable to propose that, *because imaginal cognition also plays a central role in metaphoric language and metaphoric cognition, metaphoric interventions are especially well-suited to the therapeutic task of creating new patterns and connections.* Miller (1986) offers additional support for this view, noting that:

Data from experiments on how subjects recall the verbal description of spatial relations among commonplace objects indicate the following points (Johnson-Laird, 1981; Kosslyn, 1980): (1) mental models, for example, mental images, are better remembered than propositional representations of a phenomenon; (2) we can, and often do, reason by developing [imaginal] mental models rather than strictly by syllogisms; and (3) inferences drawn from [imaginal] mental models lead to a more profound understanding of the problem situation. (p. 225)

These findings suggest that when clients are encouraged to stay within *their own* metaphors and expand and elaborate them, the meaning and insight clients gain can be more profound than if the metaphor is talked about or analyzed.

METAPHORIC STRUCTURE: THE PATTERN THAT CONNECTS

Thus far, we have seen that metaphor plays a central role in language and cognition, and that metaphor conveys meaning by integrating words and images. By extending this discussion to include Gregory Bateson's work on metaphor and "the pattern that connects," we will come to a deeper appreciation of the power of metaphor in therapy. Bateson's perspective will also enable us to understand the paradox of metaphor: that two things can be at once different and the same.

Bateson suggests that linear correspondence describes correspondence of discrete items characterized by linear, logical, cause-and-effect relations (Capra, 1988). In contrast, nonlinear correspondence describes correspondence of pattern and organization characterized by nonlinear causal chains. Thus, when causal sequences involve nonlinear correspondence, i.e., complex patterns and organization found in the living world (e.g., plants, animals, humans, families, social and cultural groups), a language other than logic is needed—a language that captures the correspondence of pattern and organization.

Linear correspondence involves a logical "if-then" relationship, such as the "Socrates Syllogism" mentioned earlier. In contrast, nonlinear correspondence is represented by Immanuel Kant's four-part analogy "a is to b as c is to d" pointing not to a resemblance between two things, but to a resemblance between two *relationships* between quite dissimilar things, i.e., "the relationship of a to b resembles that of c to d" (Campbell, 1986).

To make this more concrete, consider the example of Carol and her husband presented in the Introduction. Carol's metaphor, MY HUSBAND BARGES INTO THE HOUSE LIKE A LOCOMOTIVE, refers to Carol's experience of her estranged husband, who barges into her house without warning. As a logical relationship involving linear correspondence, the metaphor is false. It reads, "my husband is a locomotive," and if a husband is a man, then he can't be a locomotive because (among other things) men are human and locomotives are machines. As a nonlinear correspondence, however, the metaphor reads "the relationship between (a) my husband (and his behavior of entering the house without notifying me in advance), and (b) me (that is, my experience of having him do this) resembles my image of (c) a locomotive crashing through the door and careening toward (d) me (later identified as a tunnel). Thus, Carol's metaphor uses the nonlinear, "metaphoric logic," a is to b as c is to d, that is, (a) my husband is to (b) me as (c) a locomotive is to (d) a tunnel.

Let us consider another example, a woman who uses the metaphor, I'M HITTING MYSELF OVER THE HEAD WITH A HAMMER to refer to her self-critical behavior. The metaphor expresses the nonlinear correspondence of the relationship: (a) my critical self-talk and

(b) me (i.e., my "self" toward which the criticisms are directed), re-sembles (c) me holding a hammer and (d) hitting my head with it. Thus, *a* is to *b* as *c* is to *d*.

The distinction between linear and nonlinear correspondence in relation to metaphor leads to a definition of metaphoric structure that captures Bateson's concept of "the pattern that connects": *metaphoric structure identifies the pattern that connects two different things.* In this defini-tion, the "pattern that connects" is a "nonlinear" resemblance of pattern and organization between two things that are different when considered as discrete entities belonging to two different "linear" logical classes.

It should also be clear from the above discussion that linguistic metaphors reflect metaphoric structure in both language and thought (cognition).

The paradox described at the beginning of the present chapter can now be resolved. Metaphor, does, in fact, point to a resemblance between two different things. The two things compared in a metaphor *can* be both different *and* similar because their difference and similar-ity involve different levels of comparison. The fact that a metaphor is false as a *literal* statement does not address or pertain to the way in which it is true as a correspondence of similar pattern or organization.

The implications of the metaphoric pattern that connects for the unity of mind and nature will be discussed in the epilogue.

THE PATTERN THAT CONNECTS: A CLINICAL EXAMPLE

The characteristics of metaphoric structure described above are vividly demonstrated in the therapy transcript presented in Chapter 3. As the client, DJ responds to his therapist's request to explore how his early memory is similar to his current situation, he struggles to com-municate the similarities and differences. He says:

Uh hmm, yeah...I guess the snoring is pretty much the same thing that the coughing was. Well, I mean, they're different, but the effect is the same. Both are something I can't help and something that leads to me being alone. My wife left the room the other night, just like my brother did. I mean, she didn't act mad or anything, but I still felt hurt. I don't know, it was like I was being abandoned.

Snoring (the presenting problem) and coughing (the problem behavior in the early memory) are different classes of behavior (linear, logical classification) that are the same with regard to their function (the nonlinear, relational pattern that connects) in at least two ways: (1) in relation to DJ (they are both something he can't help) and (2) in DJ's relation to others (they both result in others removing themselves from him). For example, his brother's anger is different from his wife's affect (linear difference), but DJ's emotional reaction was the same; he felt hurt in relation to their leaving him in bed (nonlinear sameness).*

The concurrent similarity and difference between DJ's early memory and his current problem exemplify the metaphoric pattern that connects the early memory metaphor and the current problem. More importantly, the self-generated insight that DJ developed after he was invited to consider his *changed early recollection (ER)* as a metaphor for how he might *change the current problem* illustrates how transforming an early memory metaphor can lead to changes in thoughts, feelings, actions, and interactions in the identified problem metaphorically represented by the early recollection.

We are now in a position to apply the concepts of metaphoric language, metaphoric cognition, and metaphoric structure to the domains of social and individual reality. Drawing on the work of linguist George Lackoff and philosopher Mark Johnson, I will propose that both social and individual reality are structured metaphorically.

THE METAPHORIC STRUCTURE OF REALITY

ARGUMENT IS WAR: The Metaphoric Structure of Social Reality

In their important book, *Metaphors We Live By*, Lackoff and Johnson (1980) suggest that, based on linguistic evidence, most of our ordinary conceptual system is metaphoric in nature. They use the concept ARGUMENT and the conceptual metaphor ARGUMENT IS WAR

---

*The fact that metaphor identifies patterns and organization of relationship is the reason why the family systems therapists rely heavily on metaphor to define and change family structure (Minuchin & Fishman, 1981), to identify and change patterns of family communication (Haley, 1978; Madanes, 1981, 1984), and to train family therapists to think systemically (Duhl, 1983). These issues are discussed more fully in Chapter 11.

to illustrate how metaphors structure how we perceive, how we think, and what we do. This metaphor is reflected in our everyday language by a wide variety of expressions such as "Your claims are *indefensible*," "He *attacked every weak point* in my argument," "His criticisms were *right on target*," "I *demolished* his argument," and "He *shot down* all of my arguments" (p. 4).

The authors point out that we don't just *talk* about arguments in terms of war; we actually attack and defend, we gain and lose ground, we plan and use strategies, etc. Thus, the ARGUMENT IS WAR metaphor is a metaphor that we live by in this culture; it structures the actions we perform in arguing.

A second example of how metaphoric expression in everyday language can offer insight into the metaphoric structure of everyday activities is the metaphoric concept TIME IS MONEY. Common phrases that reflect the TIME IS MONEY metaphor include "You're *wasting* my time," "This gadget will *save* you hours," "How do you *spend* your time these days," "I've *invested* a lot of time in her," and "He's living on *borrowed* time" (Lackoff & Johnson, 1980, pp. 7, 8). These authors conclude that, because time is a valuable commodity in our culture, we understand and experience time as something that can be spent, saved, wasted, budgeted, or invested either wisely or poorly.

We may now extend our earlier observation concerning metaphoric structure. If Lackoff and Johnson are correct, not only is metaphoric structure fundamental in language and thought, *our verbal and nonverbal actions are metaphorically structured* as well. It seems clear that Lackoff and Johnson's model suggesting that social reality is structured metaphorically is consistent with the concepts of Metaphor Therapy applied in exploring and transforming client metaphors and early memories. The theory that social reality is constructed metaphorically is extended in Chapter 11 to show that family relational patterns of communication and behavior reflect the metaphoric structure of family reality, and in Chapter 7 to show that myth and archetype reflect the metaphoric structure of cultural and transcultural reality. For the present, the next task is to explore whether principles similar to those employed by Lackoff and Johnson apply when individuals use linguistic metaphors to talk about our personal feelings, relationships, life problems, etc.

I THINK, THEREFORE I AM A TEA KETTLE:
METAPHORMS AND THE METAPHORIC STRUCTURE
OF INDIVIDUAL REALITY

In Chapter 1 we were introduced to Mr. J, who, complaining that he was under "constant pressure," stated, "I feel like a tea kettle that can't let the steam out." Painting a word-picture of himself as a tea kettle, Mr. J opened a window to his inner self, into his inner world of metaphorically structured reality.

By creating the linguistic metaphor I AM A TEA KETTLE THAT CAN'T LET THE STEAM OUT, Mr. J invokes the image of a "tea kettle that can't let the steam out" to represent his self-image in relation to his current life situation. Whereas linguistic metaphors such as "He *shot down* all my arguments" emphasize a social reality, Mr. J's metaphor pertains primarily to his personal reality. Clearly, however, these two aspects of metaphoric reality are closely intertwined. In fact, as we shall see, the principles underlying Lackoff and Johnson's model of social reality may be extended to the metaphoric structure of individual reality.

Lackoff and Johnson noted that we talk about arguments using the metaphoric language of war because we think about argument in terms of the conceptual/cognitive metaphor, ARGUMENT IS WAR, and we also act the way we do in arguments for the same reason—because we think about argument in terms of the conceptual/cognitive metaphor, ARGUMENT IS WAR. Thus, metaphoric language follows from metaphoric cognition, and behavior also follows from metaphoric cognition. Similarly, Mr. J talks about himself using the linguistic metaphor "a tea kettle that can't let the steam out" because he thinks about himself in terms of the cognitive metaphor, SELF AS A TEA KETTLE (THAT CAN'T LET THE STEAM OUT). Thus, *an individual's metaphoric language reflects that individual's metaphoric cognition.*

Further, just as we have seen that conceptual metaphors such as ARGUMENT IS WAR structure our social conception, experience, and behavior in arguments, *metaphors such as I AM A TEA KETTLE represent internal metaphoric-cognitive structures that structure our personal beliefs, thoughts, feelings, behavior, and relationships in the life situation they represent.* In short, *Descartes proclaimed, "I think, therefore I am," but from*

the perspective of the metaphoric structure of reality in Metaphor Therapy, the proper statement for Mr. J in relation to his problem situation is, "I think metaphorically, therefore I am a tea kettle."
I have chosen the term *"metaphorm"** to refer to each of the six specific cognitive-metaphoric structures that comprise an individual's personality structure, i.e, the metaphoric structure of individual reality. The almost endless variety of linguistic metaphors we humans use when describing our personal reality appear to cluster around three elements and three types of relations among them. Together they comprise the six key dimensions or metaphorms of the metaphoric structure of individual reality.

Three elemental metaphorms:

- metaphorms for "self"
- metaphorms for an "other" or "others"
- metaphorms for "life"

Three relational metaphorms:

- metaphorms for self-in-relation-to-self
- metaphorms for self-in-relation-to-others
- metaphorms for self-in-relation-to-life

It is important to keep in mind that metaphorms and metaphoric structure are not intrapsychic abstractions divorced from one's social world and life situation. As we have seen, the very nature (structure) of metaphor carries meaning over from the "vehicle" or internal domain of imagination (imaginal cognition) to the "topic" or referent situation in the external world of human interaction. When Carol describes her husband as barging into the house like a locomotive, for example, the inner metaphoric image (other-metaphorm) is a locomotive, and the external referent is the husband, not as an abstract

---

*The term "metaphorm" was coined by Todd Siler (1987, 1990) who uses it to refer to the process of relating "information from one discipline to another, connecting potentially all sources and forms of information. Metaphorms are expressions of nature's unity" (Siler, 1990, p. 19). Though I prefer a more limited use of this term, in contrast to Siler's more inclusive usage, I am in full agreement that metaphor and metaphoric structure are ultimately expressions of nature's unity. This issue will be addressed in the Epilogue.

"other," but acting in a particular situational context. When Carol creates the self-metaphorm of a tunnel, this metaphoric image of self is inexorably tied to her pattern of interaction with her husband. Thus, metaphorms and the metaphoric structure of individual reality always refer to the person embedded in a social context (Adler, 1956), or, in existential terms, to one's "being-in-the-world." As Rollo May (1958) suggests, "The two poles, self and world, are always dialectically related. Self implies world and world self; there is neither without the other, and each is understandable only in terms of the other" (p. 59).

To illustrate, Table 1 presents some examples of the metaphorms that comprise the metaphoric structure of individual reality.

TABLE 1
Six Dimensions of the Metaphoric Structure of Individual Reality

METAPHORM	LINGUISTIC METAPHOR	REFERENT SITUATION
self	Self is a tea kettle about to explode	Experiencing pressure from being out of work, internal anger
other (one)	Husband is a locomotive	Estranged husband enters house at will
others (group)	Family is a jail	Teen feels constrained by parental rules and punishments
life	My life is a barren wasteland	Having no romantic relationships
self-self	Hitting myself over the head with a hammer	Self-criticism, self-sabotage of efforts
self-other	I'm trying to tame a wild lion	Wife complains that husband is reckless, impulsive, and irresponsible
self-life	I'm sinking in quicksand	Overwhelmed with workload at job, getting further behind

METAPHOR THERAPY AND THE
SENSORY WORLD OF THE INFANT

One source of support for the view that metaphor can play a powerful role in facilitating therapeutic change lies in (1) the central role of sensory imagery in metaphor, and (2) the observation that an infant's sensory imagery is already well-developed at birth and is the primary modality through which infants experience and create meaning in the world. Stern (1985), in his book *The Interpersonal World of the Infant,* discusses the infant's capacity for remembering perceptions.

Visual Perception

It is well established that infants have long-term recognition memory for visual perceptions when they reach five to seven months of age (Stern, 1985). Fagan (1973), for example, demonstrated that infants who are shown the picture of a strange person's face for less than one minute will be able to recognize the same face more than one week later.

Auditory Perception

There is evidence that an infant's auditory sensory perception begins prior to birth. For example, in a study with pregnant mothers, DeCasper and Fifer (1980) asked the mothers to talk to their fetuses during the last trimester of pregnancy, using a particular script (for example, passages from stories by Dr. Seuss). Each script had distinctive rhythmic and stress patterns. When presented with the passage they had heard in utero shortly after birth, the infants responded differently when compared to a control passage, suggesting that they recognized the passage to which they had been exposed.

Cross-Sensory Perception

Not only can infants perceive and remember individual sense modalities, they appear to have the capacity to transfer perceptual experience from one sensory modality to another.

Stern (1985) describes an experiment conducted by Meltzoff and Borton (1979) in which the experimenters blindfolded three-week-old infants and gave them one of two different pacifiers to suck on.

One pacifier had a spherical-shaped nipple and the other was a nipple with nubs protruding from various points around its surface. After the baby had some experience feeling (touching) the nipple with only the mouth, the nipple was removed and placed side by side with the other kind of nipple. The blindfold was taken off. After a quick visual comparison, infants looked more at the nipple they had just sucked. (pp. 47, 48)

Stern concludes that infants are able to perform a cross-modal transfer of information between touch and vision. This ability is a function of the innate design of the perceptual system not due to repeated world experience. Further, "The ability to perform audio-visual matching [also] appears to be well within infants' capacity by three weeks of age" (p. 49).

CONCLUSIONS

I would speculate that the *metaphoric imagery* associated with *metaphoric language/cognition* and *early memory metaphors* in Metaphor Therapy accesses the sensory-affective mode of experiential meaning that is developed very early in life. Moreover, the power of exploring and transforming metaphoric language and early memory metaphors may derive, in part, from the fact that an individual's metaphoric language and early memory metaphors access the same sensory-affective perceptual modalities that are dominant during the time when, as infants and young children, we developed our view of ourselves in relation to the world.

Thus, when a client changes his/her original metaphoric imagery or when a therapist offers a change in a client's metaphoric image that is accepted by the client, the process of therapeutic change can be hastened by a change in the client's experience of self, others, and life. Also changed are the inter-relationships between self, others, and life. Metaphoric transformations offer a novel possibility of "being-in-the-world," and therefore give the client the experience of freedom of choice. Instead of being imprisoned in the current metaphoric reality reflected in a particular metaphor or early memory metaphor, the client is freed by changing the metaphor, which can result in a change in the client's perception of reality. The changed metaphor is expanded to include a new possibility of relationship with self, others, and the world.*

Metaphorms are similar in some ways to key concepts in several theories of psychotherapy. For example, Adlerian life-style theory refers to a person's basic assumptions and images of self, others, and life, while Object Relations theory emphasizes internal representational images of self and object. The similarities and differences among these approaches and the present model will be discussed in the following chapters, where I will suggest that metaphorms and the metaphoric structure of reality can serve as a framework for integrating psychodynamic, cognitive-behavioral, and family systems therapy.

'I wish to thank Stanley Pavey, Ph.D., for helping me emphasize these points.

PART II

WEAVING THE TAPESTRY: TOWARD AN INTEGRATIVE MODEL OF METAPHOR AND PSYCHOTHERAPY

Part II examines a variety of theories and methods of psychotherapy from the perspective of Metaphor Therapy. I will suggest that metaphor is a common thread that weaves the patchwork of current psychotherapies into a coherent tapestry.

This discussion will have a dual focus. From the perspective of the different schools of therapy, the discussion will highlight the role of metaphor in each approach's theory and practice. From the perspective of Metaphor Therapy, I attempt to show that Metaphor Therapy offers a theoretical framework that identifies and integrates selected concepts and interventions from these otherwise different therapeutic approaches.

Metaphor Therapy is *not* a new "school" of therapy. The theory of Metaphor Therapy offers a different way of viewing current psychotherapies. The methods of Metaphor Therapy presented in Part I emphasize metaphoric interventions in which *client-generated* linguistic metaphors and early memory metaphors are explored and transformed. Part II expands the use of metaphor to include metaphoric interventions found in current therapy approaches that emphasize *therapist-generated* metaphors.

In contrast with the current literature that considers metaphor, if it considers it at all, mainly from within the viewpoint of a particular theory, Metaphor Therapy maintains that all theories, including theories of psychotherapy, are themselves metaphoric structures of reality. In this view, theory-based conceptual language and interpretations embody the theory's metaphoric structure of reality. In contrast, a client's metaphoric language embodies that client's metaphoric structure of individual reality. Thus, in Metaphor Therapy, theory-based interpretations are avoided because they lead away from the client's metaphoric structure of reality.

We begin with a discussion of Psychoanalytic approaches in Chapter 6, including Freud's Classical Psychoanalysis and Object Relations Theory, followed by Jung's Analytic Psychology (Chapter 7), and Milton Erickson's hypnotherapy (Chapter 8). A modified and expanded view of Cognitive-Behavior Therapy that incorporates imaginal cognition and metaphoric cognition in addition to the current emphasis on logical (syllogistic/propositional) cognition is presented in Chapter 9, followed by a discussion of Adler's Individual Psychology (Chapter 10). Strategic and Structural approaches to family systems therapy are discussed in Chapter 11. It will be suggested that the metaphoric structure of reality also applies to the family. The metaphoric structure of family reality is revealed in (1) the behavioral symptoms and the patterned interactive sequences that accompany them, (2) the verbal and nonverbal communication among family members, and (3) the family's culture. Thus, the metaphoric structure of individual and family reality are regarded as variants of the fundamental proposition, advanced in Chapter 5, that reality is structured meta-phorically. Chapter 12 presents a model of Metaphor Therapy as a framework for integrating individual and family systems approaches to psychotherapy. Part II closes with some speculations on the ways in which neuropsychological processes may mediate the therapeutic changes associated with Metaphor Therapy.

6

Metaphor Therapy and Psychoanalytic Psychotherapy

METAPHOR: INTEGRATING SECONDARY PROCESS AND PRIMARY PROCESS THINKING

Freud's concept of the unconscious is closely linked with the theory of repression and with the concept of censorship. Repression is an activity of the ego that bars from consciousness an unwanted id impulse or any of its derivatives (Brenner, 1974). Censorship refers to the defensive operations of the ego that are active during dreaming. Freud likened this function to censoring news items in the media, theorizing that the ego, in an effort to defend against the emergence into consciousness of an objectionable, repressed item, transforms the item into a disguised form—the manifest dream—which is a creation of the primary process mechanism. From the viewpoint of psychoanalysis, it is because of repression or the influence of censorship that the unconscious reveals itself in symbols or metaphors (Bettleheim, 1984).

Metaphor may be seen as lying at the interface between primary and secondary process thinking.* Secondary process thinking is the ordinary conscious form of thinking we are familiar with; it is primarily verbal and follows the usual laws of syntax and logic (Brenner, 1974). In contrast, primary process thinking uses primarily visual or other sense impressions. There is an absence of a sense of time in primary process thinking; the past, present, and future are all enfolded into one (Brenner, 1974). Also, "In primary process thinking representation by allusion or analogy is frequent and a part of an object, memory, or idea may be used to stand for the whole, or vice versa" (Brenner, 1974, pp. 48, 49).

The psychoanalytic assertion that metaphor employs both secondary *and* primary process mentation is consistent with the view (presented in Chapter 5) that metaphor integrates both word and image into a third entity characterized by "logical analogy" (Langer, 1942/ 1979) or "imaginative rationality" (Lackoff & Johnson, 1980). Also, it seems evident that secondary process thinking is similar to *logical (syllogistic/propositional) cognition* discussed in Chapter 5, while primary process thinking is similar to *imaginal cognition*. Thus, if primary process thinking is expressed mainly through the language of imagery, and secondary process is expressed mainly through words, then metaphor may be seen as an integration of primary process and secondary process thinking.

Rothenberg (1988) shares this view. He notes that "metaphor contains individually specified objects that are integrated into a larger unity with its own overall properties" (p. 41). He adds that the creation of "poetic or created" metaphors integrates two or more levels of experience. "In psychotherapy as in art and science, these levels may consist...of conscious and unconscious, of cognitive and affec-

---

*The terms "primary process" and "secondary process" are used in the psychoanalytic literature to refer to two phenomena—either as a type of thinking or as processes involved in the management of psychic energy associated with the Id and Ego, respectively (Brenner, 1974). The present discussion focuses on primary process and secondary process as modes of thinking.

tive, or of different aspects of objective reality" (Rothenberg, 1988, p. 40).

But can it be said that metaphor integrates conscious and unconscious levels of experience? Does the imagery employed by the metaphor-maker represent unconscious processes? An answer to these questions is suggested by Freud's observation that "thinking in pictures is... only a very incomplete form of becoming conscious. In some way, too, it stands nearer to unconscious processes than does thinking in words, and it is unquestionably older than the latter both ontologically and phylogenetically" (Freud, 1923/1960, p. 14). Though Freud's phrase, "thinking in pictures," emphasizes the visual sensory modality, the involvement of additional sense modalities can be inferred. Paraphrasing Freud, "Thinking in *images* stands nearer to unconscious processes than does thinking in words." Thus, it appears that metaphoric images are a form of "thinking in pictures" that are employed by the metaphor-maker to convey an experience of an issue, feeling, or situation to which the metaphor refers. It follows that metaphoric imagery, while not "unconscious," is a form of thinking through which unconscious processes are expressed.

Recall that the methods of Metaphor Therapy that explore and transform metaphoric images and images from early childhood involve a shift from thinking/communicating in words (logical cognition) to thinking/communicating in images. It may be that, from the perspective of psychoanalysis, the power of this approach lies in the fact that the client is encouraged to explore and elaborate a representation of an issue, feeling, or problem in a form of thinking (sensory imagery) that is "nearer" to unconscious processes. This view is supported by Cox and Theilgaard (1987), who suggest that imaginal communication can make contact through the defensive layer of repression by re-evoking feelings that lie below the surface.

THEORETICAL VS. CLIENT-GENERATED METAPHORS AND THE CLIENT'S UNCONSCIOUS

Freud had a preference for using metaphor in his writing and in his theorizing (Bettleheim, 1984; Edelson, 1983; Nash, 1962). Bettleheim, in his fascinating book, *Freud and Man's Soul* (1984), gives numerous examples of Freud's use of metaphor that show how Freud's emphasis on metaphor is all but lost in the English translation.

Bettleheim (1984) suggests three reasons for Freud's frequent use of metaphors in explaining the nature of psychoanalysis. First, psychoanalysis, though dealing with objective facts, employs imaginative interpretation to explain the hidden causes behind those facts, which can only be inferred. The metaphors that Freud used were intended to bridge the rift between facts and the imaginative explanation of those facts. Second, "because of repression, or the influence of censorship, the unconscious reveals itself in symbols or metaphors, and psychoanalysis, in its concern with the unconscious, tries to speak about it in its own metaphoric language" (pp. 37, 38). Finally, metaphors are able to touch a human chord and arouse our emotions, and thus, convey a feeling for what is meant. A well-chosen metaphor communicates intellectual and emotional understanding, and a true comprehension of psychoanalysis requires both; neither alone will do. Bettleheim (1984) adds that, "Because poets speak in metaphors about the content of their unconscious, Freud insisted that they, and other great artists, knew all along what he had to discover through laborious work" (p. 38).

As noted earlier, any theory is a metaphoric construction of reality. It follows that interpretations that employ theoretical concepts such as internalized objects, good and bad breast, inferiority complex, fragmented self, animus, shadow, rigid or permeable boundaries in a family, etc., use *theoretical metaphors* that reflect *the theory's metaphoric structure of reality*. From the perspective of Metaphor Therapy, a client's metaphoric language lies closer to the client's unconscious than any theory's metaphoric language. Thus, it is the metaphoric imagery *created by the person* that most directly represents that person's unconscious process. *We all are poets who speak in metaphors about the content of our unconscious.*

TRANSFERENCE AND METAPHOR

The English word "transference" derives (through the Latin) from the German word "übertragung." In the original German, however, "über" means "above or over" in English, while "tragung" means to "carry or bear." Thus, when translated into English as "carrying or bearing something from one place to another," *übertragung* includes not only the Latin meaning, "transference," but also the broader concept embodied in the Greek term "metaphor" (Szajnberg, 1985-86).

Recall that "metaphor" is derived from the Greek "meta" meaning "above or over" and "phorien" meaning "to carry or bear from one place to another." Thus, *transference actually can be translated into English as "metaphor"!*

Szajnberg (1985-86) sees transference as a subset of the larger phenomenon of metaphor. He notes that:

> Like the dream, metaphor consists of manifest meaning (the signifier), latent meaning (the signified), and particularly the creative journey between them. It is important for a psychoanalytic psychology...to recognize the component of creative work done by the individual to create a metaphor. (p. 56)

He concludes that, just as transference is a crucial aspect of the "vehicle of cure" in psychoanalytic psychotherapy, metaphor is crucial for bearing or carrying symbols and ambiguities from one time in one's life to another, from one person to another person, from one part of one's mind to another part of one's mind. The research with infants discussed in Chapter 5 appears to support Szajnberg's (1985-86) hypothesis. Linden (1985) contends that there are different levels of transference, and that not all levels meet the criteria associated with viewing transference as metaphor. In this view, metaphor captures only a part of transference. Still, one of the chief merits of dealing explicitly with transference as metaphor is that it raises primary process to the level of language (Rose, 1985-86; Siegelman, 1990).

METAPHOR AND OBJECT RELATIONS THEORY

From the perspective of Object Relations Theory, an "object" is either an external person or thing, or an internal representational image of a person, thing, or the "self." A self-object representational unit is an intrapsychic image of the other in relation to the self (Hamilton, 1988).[*]

---

[*]Like many theoretical concepts, "object" and "object relations unit" are themselves metaphors.

Siegelman (1990) proposes that, "Metaphor flows from affect because it usually represents the need to articulate a pressing inner experience of oneself and of one's internalized objects. It typically arises when feelings are high and when ordinary [literal] words do not seem strong enough or precise enough to convey the experience" (p. 16). For example, a man who was asked why he was reluctant to confront a friend about something that bothered him answered, "Because I'm afraid he'll bite my head off." In this metaphoric image, the speaker represents an aspect of his "self" as a HEAD and an aspect of the "other" as a "BITER." From the perspective of Metaphor Therapy, these representations are metaphorms, i.e., components of the speaker's metaphoric structure of individual reality. From the perspective of Object Relations theory, they can be seen as direct representations of current self-object relational units that may also represent archaic self-other relations "carried over" from childhood.

Metaphor and one's metaphoric structure of reality also express a resemblance between internal and external (interpersonal) self-object relations. Further, metaphor represents a resemblance between internal representational images of self-object relational units (another's mouth biting my head) and the external context of interpersonal self-object relations to which the metaphoric images refer (the friend and the speaker).

A client's metaphoric speech can also reveal the psychodynamics of the self. For example, patients describe the feeling of disintegration anxiety, the deepest anxiety one can experience (Kohut, 1984), using metaphors such as, "I am falling apart"; "I am lost in space without any supply of oxygen"; "I am treading water in the middle of the ocean with nothing solid to touch, no one nearby, and the ever-present danger of sharks"; or "I feel dead" (Baker & Baker, 1987).

From the viewpoint of Metaphor Therapy, each of these examples of expressions of disintegration anxiety is a metaphorm reflecting the person's metaphoric structure of individual reality. The metaphors I AM FALLING APART and I FEEL DEAD are self-self metaphorms; the metaphors I AM LOST IN SPACE WITHOUT ANY SUPPLY OF OXYGEN and I AM TREADING WATER IN THE MIDDLE OF THE OCEAN WITH NOTHING SOLID TO TOUCH, NO ONE NEARBY, AND THE EVER-PRESENT DANGER OF SHARKS are self-life metaphorms. This suggests that exploring and transforming these client metaphors using the Metaphor Therapy methods described in Chapter 1 may be regarded as exploring the

client's disintegration anxiety with the goal of reducing the experience
of disintegration and establishing a more coherent self.

METAPHORIC INTERVENTIONS IN
PSYCHOANALYTIC THERAPY

Metaphoric Interpretation

Metaphor is frequently used in psychoanalytic psychotherapy as a
vehicle for interpretation. Since a key characteristic of psychoanalytic
interpretive metaphors is that they originate with the therapist, they
will be referred to as *therapist-generated* metaphoric interventions.* In
contrast to the *client-generated* interventions described in Part I that emphasize the client's creative imagination, *therapist-generated* metaphoric
interpretations found in psychoanalytic therapy rely primarily on the
therapist's creative imagination.

In *The Creative Process of Psychotherapy*, Rothenberg (1988) applies an
understanding of the kinds of thinking involved in the creation of art,
literature, and science to psychotherapy. He focuses on the therapist's
creativity, suggesting that "it is desirable for the therapist… to function creatively in order to initiate and facilitate the patient's engage-
ment in the creative work" (p. 7). Two case examples that illustrate
Rothenberg's approach are presented later in this chapter.

Evans (1988) describes how Reider (1972) used an interpretive metaphor with a Japanese woman.

Reider's interpretive metaphor was a Japanese proverb: "A blind
man is not afraid of snakes," which he said prompted the recollection
of a dream and several sexual memories from childhood (Evans, 1988,
pp. 543-44).

Reider explains that the metaphor was effective because it allowed
the client emotional distance from the material, respected her intelli-
gence and cultural self-esteem, and integrated elements of both drive
(i.e., snakes) and defense (i.e., blindness) (Evans, 1988).

From the perspective of Metaphor Therapy, Reider's metaphoric
interpretation is effective because *it is metaphoric.* Reider reported that,
in response to hearing the phrase "A blind man is not afraid of snakes,"

---

*In fact, it appears that virtually all examples of metaphoric intervention found in the
psychotherapy literature are *therapist-generated.* These contrast with *client-generated* interventions introduced in this book.

the client recalled a dream and several sexual memories from child-hood. This suggests that the therapist's metaphoric communication engaged and activated the client's metaphoric imagery. Discussions of metaphor and the metaphoric structure of reality presented earlier suggest that Reider's metaphor, the client's dream, and the client's early childhood memories all reflect the client's metaphoric structure of individual and cultural reality.

Unfortunately, any inferences about *the client's* metaphoric imagery in Reider's case example are speculative due to the absence of tran-script data and other specific information concerning the client's re-sponse to the therapist's metaphoric interpretation. The absence of this material in Reider's report may be due to the emphasis on *the therapist's* use of metaphor and for the preference in psychoanalysis to describe the client's process using psychoanalytic concepts.

Perhaps an even more likely explanation derives from the psycho-analytic view (Aleksandrowicz, 1962; Ekstein, 1966) that metaphor arises in psychotherapy as a regressive phenomenon. For example, Ekstein (1966) notes that "The use of metaphor...must not be regarded as a treatment technique in itself. It is but a preliminary approxima-tion to the final therapeutic act which ultimately consists of a classical interpretation at the level of secondary process" (p. 158).

Seen from the viewpoint of Metaphor Therapy, explaining the ef-fectiveness of metaphoric interventions based on theoretical constructs such as "drives" and "defenses," regarding metaphor as "regressive," and seeing metaphoric communication as preliminary and subordi-nate to conceptual interpretation based on classical psychoanalytic theory all reflect the potential bias in psychoanalysis that can lead to translating indigenous metaphoric communication into theoretical metaphors. The main thrust of the present argument calls for an em-phasis on the client's metaphoric imagery and the client's metaphoric structure of reality. However, when therapist-generated metaphors are used effectively, their effectiveness derives from the fact that they engage the client's inner metaphoric processes, i.e., the client's meta-phoric, sensory imagery.

Evans (1988) offers the following critique of the psychoanalytic per-spective discussed above:

The dualistic psychoanalytic distinction between primary process fantasy and secondary process "reality oriented" thinking obscures the role of metaphoric language in the construction of one's experiential world. This latter view regarding the epistemically creative function of metaphor is suggested by theories which argue that novel metaphors generate new meanings that cannot be expressed in literal terms. The perils of this psychoanalytic dualism is further seen in the fact that a literal psychoanalytic interpretation often involves a reification of one of its own conceptual metaphors....Thus, one limitation in the psychoanalytic understanding of metaphor is that it is not metaphorical enough, not sufficiently aware of its own use of metaphor. (p. 544)

Evans' emphasis on the creative function of metaphor and his call for greater awareness of the metaphoric nature of psychoanalytic interpretation are consistent with the thrust of the present argument. As noted above, however, some psychoanalysts reject the dualistic view. For example, Rothenberg (1988) views metaphor as combining primary and secondary process thinking, and emphasizes the creative role of metaphor. The following two case examples illustrate this approach.

Metaphoric Interpretation of Behavioral Symptoms: The Benefit of Being a Sleepwalker

Rothenberg (1988), in his important book, *The Creative Process in Psychotherapy*, presents a case that illustrates how therapists can use metaphor to interpret behavioral symptoms. One example involves a 21-year-old male who suffered with symptoms of depersonalization, withdrawal, and an inability to concentrate. During one therapy session, the client reported that his girlfriend was constantly angry and woke him up three times each night. When the therapist suggested that being awakened frequently and the client's feelings about this might be the reason he was not sleeping, the client responded: "I have no feelings; I'm in a daze all the time" (p. 43). At this point the therapist offered an interpretive metaphor: "Well, the benefit of being a sleepwalker is that you don't have to know or feel, but you can still move around and participate in what goes on" (p. 43). Rothenberg (1988) noted that the patient responded positively, indicating that he didn't allow himself to have feelings because he felt he didn't *deserve* to have them. "For the remainder of the session, he productively pursued the important theme, for him, of the difficulty and danger of both having and expressing feelings" (p. 43).

Rothenberg's intervention demonstrates that therapist-generated metaphoric interpretations can be powerful when they "connect" with and are accepted by the client. In the above example, the client accepts the metaphoric representation of self, I AM A SLEEPWALKER. This illustrates an important point: *those metaphoric interpretations that aim at capturing the client's experience and meaning in the language of the client without going beyond what the client has presented have the greatest potential of being accepted by the client.*

Note that, from the viewpoint of Metaphor Therapy, the client would also be encouraged to explore and transform the metaphor of SELF AS SLEEPWALKER, a process that would more actively and directly engage the client's "primary process" sensory imagery. By inviting the client to transform the metaphoric image of himself as a sleepwalker, the therapist would offer an opportunity for the client to create in the domain of metaphor a potential solution to the problem he is experiencing in his life. Even where the client's transformation is less than ideal, it offers important insight into the client's hopes and expectations regarding what is possible and/or desirable within his subjective frame of reference.

As mentioned above, in order to be effective, therapist-generated metaphoric interpretations must create a metaphor that accurately captures the experience and dynamics of the client so that the client's metaphoric cognitive and neuropsychological processes are engaged. In contrast, exploring and transforming the metaphoric imagery created by the client *directly engages* the client's metaphoric cognitive processes. The therapist's role in the latter intervention is mainly to guide and facilitate the process. In explore/transform metaphor methods, the client generates most of the imagery while the therapist guides the exploration and invites the transformation. This ensures that metaphoric imagery reflects the client's experience. Also, the client "owns" the process because the metaphoric imagery comes from within.

Organ Jargon—Metaphoric Interpretation of Physical Symptoms: She Really Gets Under Your Skin

Adler (1956) maintained that the mouth may lie, the mind may fail to understand, but the body always tells the truth. Thus, from an Adlerian point of view, physical symptoms are an important form of psychological communication that Adler called "organ jargon." Interpretive metaphors can put this body-talk into words. This is illustrated in Albert Rothenberg's work with a 25-year-old female patient who entered treatment because of a skin rash covering her hands and forearms. Rothenberg (1988) reports that a physical examination found no physiological basis for the rash. The patient began the fourth session expressing mild disappointment concerning something her older sister had done and said to her. The therapist responded with the metaphoric interpretation, "She really gets under your skin, doesn't she" (p. 45). The patient acknowledged that she felt intense anger toward her sister.

When, several weeks later, the patient suggested that in some ways her sister's personality resembled that of the patient's mother, the therapist remarked, "She [the mother] gets under your skin, too, doesn't she" (p. 45). In response, the patient acknowledged some ambivalent feelings toward her mother that previously she had denied. Rothenberg identifies this metaphoric interpretation as a turning point in the treatment "because, following the session, the patient's skin ailment began to improve noticeably, and as the therapy progressed she became increasingly comfortable in discussing her ambivalent feelings and underlying conflict regarding her mother" (p. 45).

From Rothenberg's psychoanalytic viewpoint, the symptom may be "caused" by unexpressed conflict and repressed ambivalent feelings. From the perspective of Adlerian theory, the symptom is an expression of the holistic, self-consistent unity of the client's life style and communicates in somatic language (organ jargon) the client's irritation with her sister and mother. According to Metaphor Therapy, this case illustrates how the body "speaks" in the language of metaphors and how physical symptoms can express nonverbal metaphoric communication.* It would seem, therefore, that *both mind and body are unified within the metaphoric structure of individual reality.*

METAPHOR THERAPY AND DANIEL STERN'S "KEY THERAPEUTIC METAPHOR"

According to Stern (1985), the fundamental task of psychoanalytic therapy is for the therapist and client to search through the client's

---

*Somatic-metaphoric communication may be considered another form similar to the nonlinear, imagistic, gestural communication discussed in Chapter 5 (McNeill, 1992).

remembered history and find "the key therapeutic metaphor for understanding and changing the patient's life" (p. 257).

CASE EXAMPLE: WAITING FOR THE WORLD TO BEGIN

Stern illustrates this approach with a professional woman in her thirties who felt unable to cope by herself or to initiate her own wishes and goals. She felt paralyzed in her law career and felt she had no control over her present situation and that her life was in the hands of others.

The narrative point of origin was determined to be the time when she was largely bedridden with rheumatic fever and subacute bacterial endocarditis between eight and 10 years of age. She had been ordered not to move about and she was too physically fatigued to do anything. Thus, she had to wait for her mother or father to make anything happen.

This example highlights several similarities and differences between Stern's psychoanalytic approach and Metaphor Therapy. In Metaphor Therapy, the therapist and client search for something akin to a life-experience in the client's "remembered history." However, since Metaphor Therapy focuses more heavily on identifying and changing the client's metaphoric structure of reality than on actual historical life events, a therapist guided by this (Metaphor Therapy) approach would attend to the metaphoric communication of the client and seek to elicit specific early memory metaphors related to current problems and issues.

For example, Stern noted that the most acute source of suffering for his client was "her sense of paralysis in her law career," and that she felt that "her life was in the hands of others." It is not clear from Stern's report whether these metaphors originate with him or with his client—a point of central importance from the viewpoint of Metaphor Therapy. If these metaphors were created by the client, the therapist would invite the client to explore and eventually transform them. While both metaphors use somatic sensory imagery, the paralysis metaphor is especially interesting in light of the client's focus on physical acts, and her subsequent revelation of her virtual paralysis while bedridden as a child. For example, the therapist might say, "You said you have a sense of paralysis in your law career. What image comes to your mind when you think of this sense of paralysis?" Also, since the experience of being bedridden occurred over a period of two years, the Metaphor Therapy approach would seek to elicit specific early recollections that took place during this period. It is interesting to speculate on the potential therapeutic impact of using Metaphor Therapy methods with this client. For example, would therapy be deepened and/or accelerated if one encouraged her to explore the metaphors of paralysis in her law career and life being in the hands of others, and elicited early memory metaphors associated with these metaphoric images?

7

Metaphor Therapy and Jung's Analytic Psychology

Although Jung rarely referred to metaphor himself, others (e.g., Siegelman, 1990; Young-Eisendrath & Hall, 1991) have discussed the importance of metaphor in Jung's Analytic Psychology.

Perhaps the chief similarity between Metaphor Therapy and Analytic Psychology is the central role that sensory imagery plays in both approaches. Young-Eisendrath and Hall (1991) note that, for Jung, the emotionally infused image is the primary organizer of the human psyche. Their explanation of Jung's emphasis on imagery and imagination includes several points in common with Metaphor Therapy: (1) the period in which image-thinking predominates is developmentally prior to the mastery of syntax and in language; (2) these images are assumed to be more motivating, more powerful, than any attempt to render them in language; (3) their meaning cannot be fully encompassed by language and rational forms of thought; and (4) "Images may lead to emotionally based organizations of thought, metaphoric models that eventually develop into representations of complex emotionally motivating schematic meanings" (pp. 2, 3). These metaphoric models, also represented in Jung's concepts of active imagination, symbol, and dreams, seem consistent with Metaphor Therapy's concepts of metaphorms and the metaphoric structure of individual reality.

ARCHETYPE AND MYTH: THE METAPHORIC STRUCTURE OF TRANSCULTURAL REALITY

Young-Eisendrath and Hall (1991) point out that archetype means "primary imprint" indicating "a universal disposition to construct an image, usually in an emotionally aroused state" (pp. 1, 2). For example, these authors note that the archetype of the self "can be considered a universal metaphor that is used to map invariants of subjectivity back and forth between embodied experiences of oneself and inferred experiences of other selves..." (p. 24).

Joseph Campbell's extensive study of mythology and religion supports the view that myth and archetype are universal metaphoric images. Campbell (1986) suggests that the systematic comparison of myths and religions requires us to (1) identify the universals (archetypes), and (2) "recognize and interpret the various locally and historically conditioned transformations of the metaphorical images through which these universals have been rendered" (p. 99).

Campbell (1986) adds that "Every myth..., whether or not by intention, is *psychologically* symbolic. Its narratives and images are to be read, therefore, not literally, but as metaphors" (emphasis in original) (p. 55).

Taken together, both Jung's concept of archetype, understood as a "universal metaphor," and Campbell's insight that myths in human culture reveal universal metaphoric images, suggest that *myth and archetype point to a universal dimension of human experience—the metaphoric structure of transcultural reality.*

Recall that metaphoric thinking points to resemblance of pattern between different things. *Applied to human culture, the metaphoric perspective points to universal, transcultural "patterns that connect"* * *(Bateson, 1979) each of us as members of the community of humankind, while preserving the diversity of differences that make each culture unique.*

MYTH AND METAPHOR: CULTURAL AND PERSONAL DIMENSIONS

Rollo May offers an additional perspective on myth that is of particular interest to the present discussion. Citing Jung and Campbell, May (1991) notes that the deepest archetypal level of the unconscious is discovered through myth. "Each of us, by virtue of our pattern of myths, participates in these archetypes; they are the structure of human existence" (p. 38), and "They are narrations by which our society is unified" (p. 20).

Recall that May (1991) also suggests that personal myths can be discerned in a person's earliest childhood memories, and that "Memory and myth are inseparable..." (p. 70).

Viewed from the perspective of Metaphor Therapy, May's concept of personal myth suggests that personal myths are being engaged and transformed when one explores and transforms early memory metaphors. Further, by emphasizing both (1) the personal myths of the unique individual (what Adler [1956] called the "guiding fiction" of the individual, which is a synonym for myth [May, 1991]) and (2) the universal pattern of myths across cultures, May suggests a resemblance and continuity between the unique and the universal structure of human existence. Given the metaphoric nature of myth discussed earlier, May's view appears consistent with Metaphor Therapy's proposition that individual, social, and transcultural reality is structured metaphorically.

Thus, each of us develops a personal mythology that is reflected in our personal "guiding fiction," i.e., the metaphoric pattern that connects and makes sense of our experience of the world. Our personal

---

*Bateson's concept of "the pattern that connects" is discussed more fully in the Epilogue.

mythic reality—our own metaphoric structure of individual reality—is revealed in our early memory metaphors.

Perhaps understanding intrapersonal and transcultural myths would help us see both the universal and the unique in others. This understanding may help us to embrace the similarities that connect and unify us within the family of humankind while helping us to appreciate the differences that make us unique.

8

Metaphor Therapy and Ericksonian Hypnotherapy

SOME SHARED ASSUMPTIONS

Milton Erickson pioneered the use of stories and anecdotes as metaphors in therapy. While the Ericksonian approach differs in most respects from psychodynamic approaches, the Ericksonian rationale for the use and power of metaphoric stories, anecdotes, and multiple embedded metaphors in promoting therapeutic change rests, in part, on the concepts of unconscious and conscious process.

For Milton Erickson, "unconscious" refers to any process that lies outside the awareness of the personality, but which plays a role in determining conscious and bodily phenomena (Lankton & Lankton, 1983). Erickson maintained that much of unconscious experience is nonverbally expressed. He saw neurotic symptoms as behavior that is defensive and protective, and as an unconscious process that is excluded from conscious understandings (Lankton & Lankton, 1983).

Erickson's view of unconscious and conscious process, and of neurotic symptoms, is reminiscent of the psychodynamic perspectives discussed above.* His use of paradox in therapy is also based on these premises. For example, in response to paradoxical interventions such as "'Don't give up your faults...you're going to need them to understand your spouse's,' [and] 'And, look forward to the days when you can look back'" (Lankton & Lankton, 1983, p. 67). Lankton and Lankton (1983) point out that:

> The client's conscious mind is temporarily overloaded by the illogical logic of the paradoxical communication and the first subjective mental state is confusion, the client is in a process of mental search. Such mental search is an adaptive function and probably is best characterized by the concept of primary process activity.... As the conscious mind begins the search, so does the unconscious mind. (p. 67)

This passage reflects several points of correspondence between Ericksonian theory and Metaphor Therapy. First, the mental search stimulated by the therapist's paradoxical communication is described as unconscious, primary process activity, which Metaphor Therapy identifies as imaginal cognition utilizing sensory imagery. Second, the view that both conscious and unconscious processes participate in the mental search seems consistent with the process associated with exploring and transforming client metaphors and early memory metaphors, and Metaphor Therapy's view that metaphor integrates unconscious and conscious processes.

---

*This view is especially close to Adler's Individual Psychology discussed in Chapter 10. Like Erickson, Adler (1956) rejected Freud's "drive-structure" model (Greenberg & Mitchell, 1983), opting instead to regard unconscious process as the "not understood," i.e., that which is outside one's awareness.

METAPHORIC ANECDOTES

The primary use of metaphor in Ericksonian therapy is in the form of stories and anecdotes. Lankton and Lankton (1983) point out that the technical differences between stories, anecdotes, and metaphors are of no concern in Ericksonian therapy. In fact, the great popularity of Ericksonian approaches has led many therapists to consider metaphoric anecdotes and stories as the only or the primary approach to using metaphor in therapy. Nonetheless, the Ericksonian approach of using therapist-constructed stories, anecdotes, and multiple embedded metaphors is a unique and important contribution to the repertoire of metaphoric methods available to the therapist.

CASE EXAMPLE: THE DAYS OF RETIREMENT AND ROSES

Anecdotal metaphors are used for a wide range of purposes and can become quite complex in structure and in the variety of multiple metaphors embedded within an anecdote (see, for example, Barker, 1985; Gordon, 1978; Lankton & Lankton, 1983, 1989). Lankton and Lankton (1983) illustrate and explain the anecdotal metaphor method, using multiple embedded metaphors with a woman who is not finding satisfaction in retirement. These authors indicate that they might discuss "aspects of a rose from bud to full bloom, eventually unfolding its petals, producing seed and being suspended in full beauty for the enjoyment of the environment and its owner prior to the final cyclical demise" (p. 90), as a way of addressing her upcoming retirement and other issues related to her stage of social development. Their rationale is that finding satisfaction in retirement after engaging in a career is parallel to the life cycle of a rose, which ends with the mature flower "having survived to bring pleasure and seed, dies proudly in order to assist the development of the new growth on the bush" (p. 90).

The Lanktons report that this metaphoric anecdote helped the client examine ideas related to finding satisfaction outside her normal framework. By "reordering priorities in the metaphor about the rose, she could also consider her satisfactions and the importance of fulfilling goals outside her current framework of dissatisfaction" (p. 90).

COMPARISON OF ERICKSONIAN AND
METAPHOR THERAPY APPROACHES

Ericksonian and Metaphor Therapy approaches share a common goal of using metaphor to communicate with and activate the client's unconscious processes. Like explore/transform interventions introduced in Part I, Ericksonian anecdotes and multiple embedded metaphors seek to create a shift in the client's cognitive mode of processing information from primarily verbal-logical to imaginal-analogical cognition. However, Ericksonian methods differ from interventions that explore and transform client metaphors in several important ways.

First, in Ericksonian therapy the therapist constructs relatively complex anecdotes and stories containing metaphors and submetaphors designed to parallel the client's situation and subjective world view. In contrast, explore/transform methods encourage clients to create out of their own creative imagination a scenario whose starting point is the clients' metaphoric language or early childhood memory. Although both approaches utilize the client's creative imagination, Ericksonian interventions employ a primarily *indirect* path to this goal. With explore/transform methods, the path is relatively *direct.*

Second, the Ericksonian therapist uses metaphoric anecdotes to achieve a specific goal based on a treatment plan or therapeutic objective. Lankton and Lankton's book, *Tales of Enchantment: Goal-Oriented Metaphors for Adults and Children in Therapy* (1989), presents a cornucopia of therapeutic "tales of enchantment" designed to achieve specific therapeutic goals. In contrast, explore/transform methods are relatively open-ended and unstructured. Thus, the role of the therapist is to aid the client in exploring client-generated metaphors. In this sense, it is the therapist who follows the client's lead, rather than the other way around. As noted earlier, therapists following this approach may also, in accordance with the client's dynamics, invite the client to consider alternate reframes (transformations) of the client's metaphors, as well as offering metaphors of their own.

Finally, Ericksonian use of metaphoric stories and anecdotes has the same requirements as other therapist-generated metaphoric interventions, namely, their effectiveness depends on the therapist's accurate empathy, clinical sensitivity and intuition, and creative imagination, as well as on extensive training and experience.

9

Metaphor Therapy and Cognitive-Behavior Therapy

Virtually all cognitive-behavioral approaches rely almost exclusively on the propositional/syllogistic form of cognition when formulating a client's cognitions, (e.g., self-talk, automatic thoughts, and irrational beliefs) and cognitive schemas. Metaphor Therapy broadens the concept of "cognition" to include the imaginal and metaphoric forms of cognition in addition to propositional/syllogistic or "logical" cognition. The implications of viewing cognitive-behavior therapy from this tridimensional model of cognition are explored in this section.

THE CENTRAL ROLE OF LOGICAL COGNITION IN
CURRENT COGNITIVE-BEHAVIOR THERAPIES

Cognitive-Behavior Therapy (CBT) focuses on conscious thoughts in contrast to unconscious processes. Initially, Beck (1976) emphasized "cognitive events," which he defined as a thought, reminiscence, or image occurring in the "free-flowing stream of consciousness," as the primary focus of cognitive therapy.

Sometimes called "automatic thoughts" (Beck, 1976), "self-talk" and "internal dialogue" (Meichenbaum, 1977), or the "hidden reason" (Dreikurs, 1973), these cognitions usually occur outside awareness but may be brought into awareness if one asks a client to report what the client said to him/herself at a particular moment in time.

Beck et al. (1979) later extended the theory and practice of cognitive therapy, emphasizing *cognitive schemas* as well as cognitions. Cognitive schemas are attitudes or assumptions developed from previous experiences on which cognitions are based. Beck illustrated the nature and relationship of automatic thoughts (i.e., cognitions) and cognitive schemas with the case of a 33-year-old depressed woman with two children. Her most recent depression coincided with her recent divorce, at which time she moved from a rural to an urban setting. Her children were having trouble adjusting to the new area. The client's cognitive schema included assumptions such as: "If I'm nice (suffer for others, appear bright and beautiful) bad things (divorce, rambunctious children) won't happen to me," and "It is my fault when bad things happen (because I wasn't nice)." Her automatic thoughts include "I caused my husband to behave badly," "I ruined my children's lives by getting a divorce," "I never have good times," and "It's because I am not nice" (Beck et al., 1979, pp. 249-251).

Although he includes images in his definition of a cognitive event, in practice Beck and most other CBT practitioners emphasize *logical cognition* (i.e., verbal/logical statements that move from premise to conclusion) when formulating a client's cognitions and cognitive schemas of dysfunctional assumptions or irrational beliefs. These dysfunctional assumptions function as rules by which the person attempts to make sense of the world, as well as acting to predispose a person to depression. Beck et al. (1979) note that "Such characteristic thinking aberrations as exaggeration, overgeneralization, and absoluteness are built into the framework of the rule and, consequently, press the person to make an exaggerated, overgeneralized, absolute conclusion" (p. 100). Beck adds that these rules are applied as though in a syllogism:

Major Premise: "If I don't have love, I am worthless."
Special Case: "Raymond doesn't love me."
Conclusion: "I am worthless." (p. 100)

Similarly, Ellis (1989) states that Rational-Emotive Therapy teaches clients "how to dispute irrational ideas and inappropriate behaviors and to internalize rules of logic and scientific method" (p. 199).

Cognitive-Behavior Therapy's emphasis on logical cognition is consistent with its focus on verbal (in contrast to imaginal or metaphoric) language and cognition, since, as noted earlier in Chapter 5, linear, sequential, verbal communication is associated with syllogistic/logical cognition.

It should be noted that some CBT approaches, such as Lazarus' Multimodal Therapy (Lazarus, 1976, 1978, 1989) and Wolpe's (1958) systematic desensitization technique, employ imagery as part of their approach. These are exceptions rather than the rule, however. Also, like the CBT approaches discussed above, these methods do not employ metaphoric interventions.

CONCLUSION

The above discussion is not meant as a criticism of CBT; its value and efficacy have been proven beyond question. This raises an interesting question: What are the similarities and differences of CBT methods compared to Metaphor Therapy methods? Are the mechanisms of change similar or different for the two approaches?

At present, there appears to be no clear answer to this question, and further understanding will have to await empirical investigation. It would seem reasonable to expect that the mechanisms of change may differ because humans utilize logical-syllogistic, imaginal, and metaphoric modes of cognition to understand their experience and their world. The form or combination of forms of cognition that would be most effective in any particular case may depend on a variety of variables, such as the problem, the family and social context, the person, the dynamics, the preferred cognitive style of the person, and the person's psychological, physiological, and neuropsychological strengths and weaknesses. On the other hand, CBT and Metaphor Therapy share some characteristics. Both approaches aim at identifying and changing the way in which people organize their experience and create meaning in the world. Thus, both are relatively "close to the data," and attempt to capture and respond to the uniqueness of the individual.

The goal of the present discussion is to place CBT in a broader context. Noting that current approaches to CBT tend to emphasize the logical-syllogistic form of cognition suggests that two additional cognitive modalities–imaginal cognition and metaphoric cognition– may be considered important dimensions of cognitive therapy that to date have been underemphasized. This scheme would incorporate and integrate both logical and imaginal cognition as a "3-dimensional" form of cognitive therapy.

In addition, based on the comparative analysis of metaphor therapy and psychodynamic therapy presented above, this scheme may offer a framework within which psychodynamic concepts and methods that emphasize unconscious processes expressed symbolically through sensory affective imagery (i.e., imaginal and metaphoric cognition) may be regarded as different yet compatible when compared with CBT concepts and methods that emphasize cognitive processes expressed in self-talk, cognitive schemas, and beliefs (i.e., logical, syllogistic/propositional cognition).

10

Metaphor Therapy and Adler's Individual Psychology

Many of the concepts found in CBT bear striking similarity to Alfred Adler's Individual Psychology. Considered a forerunner of modern cognitive therapies (Ellis, 1973, 1989; Murray & Jacobson, 1978), Adler maintained that one's opinions and beliefs were the primary determiners of behavior. In the following passage, originally published in 1933, Adler stated that:

> I am convinced that a person's behavior springs from his opinion. We should not be surprised at this, because our senses do

not receive actual facts, but merely a subjective image of them, a reflection of the external world.... It has the same effect on me whether a poisonous snake is actually approaching my foot or whether I merely believe that it is a poisonous snake. (Adler, 1956, p. 182)

LIFE STYLE: THE UNIFYING PATTERN OF PERSONALITY

A person's life style (Adler's term for personality) is a cognitive blueprint for behavior, the "rule of rules" for the individual (Shulman, 1973). Further, the life style organizes these cognitive rules, feelings, and behaviors into a *unifying pattern.*

The life style is comprised of one's basic assumptions, beliefs, images, and/or expectations about self, life, others; one's fictional goal; and the behavioral methods the person uses to overcome subjectively defined feelings of inadequacy and insecurity by moving toward a subjectively defined goal/self-ideal of significance and security. Shulman (1973) offers two examples typical of an Adlerian formulation of a person's life-style beliefs:

Example 1:
   I am small and weak.
   Life is dangerous.
   Therefore others must protect me.

Example 2:
   I am the rightful heir to my father's power.
   Life is here to appreciate me and serve me.
   Therefore, I have to be the center of attention. (p. 25)

Clearly, these formulations employ the syllogistic, logical form of cognition also used by Beck and other cognitive-behavior therapists.

Life Style and Metaphor

While Adlerians usually conceptualize life-style dynamics using syllogistic/propositional cognition, life style is also represented in imaginal and metaphoric cognitive modalities. This is consistent with Adler's concept of "the schema of apperception," which is associated with analogical in contrast to logical processes. According to Adler (1956), "All cognition is the apperception of one thing through another. In understanding, we are always dealing with an analogy.... All conception and cognition are based upon analogical apperceptions" (p. 79).

Like the metaphoric structure of individual reality in Metaphor Therapy, life style may be represented by sensory images of self, life, and others, and organized around a person's self-ideal image or imaginal representation of his or her life-style goal.* Another point of convergence between Metaphor Therapy and Adlerian therapy is the use of early childhood memory images (early recollections) to identify life-style themes (Adler, 1956; Ansbacher, 1946; Baruth & Eckstein, 1978; Mosak, 1958; Mosak & Kopp, 1973; Olson, 1979; Shulman & Mosak, 1988).

One important difference between Adlerian and Metaphor therapies is that Adlerians typically use early recollections as a basis for interpretation of a client's life-style beliefs and goals, a process that involves translating the image recalled from childhood into a logical-syllogistic form representing the client's basic assumptions, beliefs, and goals. In contrast, a therapist following the Metaphor Therapy approach would emphasize using the early recollection as a direct representational image of current issues and subjective meaning.

The Creative Imagination in Adlerian Therapy: Working with Dream Imagery

There are a few important exceptions to this emphasis on syllogistic cognition in Adlerian therapy. Some Adlerians employ therapeutic methods that do emphasize imaginal and metaphoric cognitive processes. These include dreamwork (Gold, 1978, 1988), art therapy (S. Dreikurs, 1986), and psychodrama (Star, 1977). Like the metaphoric methods described earlier, these approaches focus on engaging the client's creative imagination (Kopp, Gold, & Pew, 1992).

Gold's (1988) approach to dream interpretation and dream therapy illustrates this dimension of Adlerian therapy. He uses the dream as

---

*Adler (1956) regards the life-style goal as the principle of internal, subjective causation of psychological events. It is a creation of the individual that is largely unconscious and represents the unity and self-consistency of the personality structure.

an entrance into the subjective world of the dreamer. He emphasizes imaginal in contrast to logical cognition, noting that the use of inner imagery permits the client to create new perspectives that facilitate change in attitudes resulting in changes in life.

The main thrust of Gold's method is illustrated in his work with a single woman in her forties. Gold (1988) reports that she is professionally and economically successful, tends to be overly responsible, is unappreciated, especially by her family, and suffers from low self-esteem. She reported feeling depressed for many years. In her third session of treatment she reported the following dream:

"I am in a flower garden. The weather is pleasant but I am feeling very uncomfortable. As I am pacing up and down I look over to the center of the garden. There is a black cube. It frightens me and at the same time I feel very angry. I don't like it. It doesn't belong there and yet it dominates everything. I wake up." She then looks at the therapist and says, "Now don't ask me what it means. I haven't the vaguest idea." (p. 48)

Gold (1988) interprets the dream as follows:

My life (the garden) should be happier, but there are things I cannot see or understand (the black cube) which spoil it. I am a victim and helpless because I don't know why it is there (Don't ask me what it means). (p. 48)

Thus far, Gold's approach follows along traditional Adlerian lines, interpreting the dream "as one interprets poetry." The dream and its symbols are understood as metaphors. However, the interpretation (of what Adlerians consider the person's "private logic" or "schema of apperception") is formulated through logical/propositional forms ("My life should be...but...," "I am...because...").

Typically, the next step for most Adlerian therapists would be to offer the interpretation to the client and explore the client's responses to the interpretation. Gold (1988) takes a different tack, and in doing so demonstrates an Adlerian intervention that emphasizes imaginal cognitive processes. Focusing on the black cube as a symbol of her strong emotions that underlay her depression, he asked the dreamer to imagine the cube is in front of her. Next, the therapist asked her what would happen if he opened the cube. Indicating that he had opened the cube, he asked what she sees when she looks in. She replied, "snakes." When asked what happens to the snakes once the cube is open, she said that they disappeared into the garden.

The therapist then asked the client if it would be all right to have all the snakes back in the open cube for a moment. She agreed, and the therapist indicated he was going to reach into the cube and pick up a snake and show it to her. When asked if it reminded her of anything, she said it reminded her of her mother. As the therapist removed one snake after another she named her siblings, her father, and others who were close to her. Finally, when the therapist asked the client how come the snakes, when let out of the cube, simply disappeared into the garden without hurting her, she said:

> I guess if I were perfectly honest with myself, they never really hurt me. They could get angry with me because of my bossy ways. I know my mother loved me. Maybe I wanted too much from her. She is not a terrible person. In fact she is rather nice. It's my wanting to be the favorite that gets me into difficulty. (p. 50)

The therapist invites the client to explore and elaborate the dream symbol within the realm of her sensory imagination. Asking the client what would happen if the therapist opened the cube and asking permission to put the snakes back in the cube indicate that Gold's style is more directive compared with the explore/transform methods presented in Part I. Still, Gold's method emphasizes client-generated imagery and content and avoids conceptual interpretation. The connections and insight are generated by the client. Also, the dream symbol serves as a starting point for the client to generate new imagery (snakes that disappear into the garden) similar to the type generated by clients when they explore and transform a metaphoric image.

This example of dream therapy highlights the difference between dreams and metaphors. Metaphor is a bridge between the domain of internal imagery and the domain of external life in which an image is used to convey meaning about a situation. In order for a metaphor to be a true metaphor, there must be a resemblance between two parts, the metaphoric image and the referent topic to which it refers. In contrast, the dream and dream symbols are images whose referents are not yet clear. They are "metaphors-in-waiting." Dream symbols become true metaphors only when the thing(s) to which they refer are identified. For example, the image of the snakes that emerged as the client explored what she saw inside the black cube became a meta-phor (metaphoric image) only when the client identified the snakes as representing various people she knew. The therapist invited the client to create a metaphor from an image when he asked if the snakes re-minded the client of anything.

In sum, Gold's approach to dream therapy demonstrates an Adlerian method of working with imaginal representations of private logic and life style in which insight and change are stimulated using imaginal and metaphoric cognition.

11

Metaphor Therapy and Family Systems Therapy

The purpose of this chapter is to discuss selected concepts and methods of Structural and Strategic Family Therapy from the perspective of Metaphor Therapy. Both Structural and Strategic approaches offer models of the family system that support Metaphor Therapy's view that family reality is structured metaphorically. In addition, Strategic and Structural Family Therapies extend the repertoire of metaphor methods available to the therapist by offering intervention strategies that identify and transform family structure and communication/interaction patterns.

Finally, I will suggest that the metaphoric structure of family reality, while differing from the metaphoric structure of individual reality in some important respects, shares many basic constructs and approaches to therapeutic change.

METAPHOR THERAPY AND STRUCTURAL FAMILY THERAPY

The Metaphoric Structure of Family Reality: Contributions of Structural Family Therapy

According to Minuchin and Fishman (1981), the family constructs its present reality, and it is the therapist's task to select "from the family's own culture the metaphors that symbolize their narrowed reality," and use them "as a label that points up the family reality and suggests the direction for change" (p. 227).

Thus, Structural Family Therapy's theory appears consistent with three premises of Metaphor Therapy: (1) the family constructs its reality; (2) "family structure" is metaphoric in nature; and, (3) the therapist uses metaphor in therapy to suggest directions for change.

Metaphoric Interventions: Identifying and Changing the Metaphoric Structure of Family Reality

CASE EXAMPLE # 1: THE FAMILY IS A TRAP

Minuchin (Minuchin & Fishman, 1981) consulted with a family in which the father/husband was depressed. During the session, Minuchin asked Mother whether Father communicates his feelings. Mother indicated that sometimes Father would "blurt out" his feelings while at other times he "keeps it in because I get upset when he brings it out" (p. 35). She added that it depended on whether or not he could cope with her reaction of being upset. Father said that he holds his irritation in until "some little thing" triggers a reaction, at which time he becomes "very, very critical and get[s] angry" (p. 36). When Father added, "But then I try to be very careful not to be unreasonable or too harsh because when I'm harsh, I feel guilty about it," Minuchin responded, "So, sometimes the family feels like a trap" (p. 36).

Minuchin responded to Father's and Mother's description by introducing the metaphor, THE FAMILY IS A TRAP, to identify the family's metaphoric structure of reality.

CASE EXAMPLE # 2: MOTHER IS HER SON'S ALARM CLOCK

In this example, Minuchin introduced a metaphor to capture the metaphoric structure of reality in a dyadic subsystem involving a mother and her son, Bud.

Minuchin (Minuchin & Fishman, 1981) asked Bud, who has difficulty getting up in the morning, if an alarm clock would solve the problem. When Bud said he has an alarm clock of his own, Minuchin asked, "Do you have an alarm clock, or is mother an alarm clock?" Bud denied that his mother was his alarm clock, but when Minuchin asked him who wakes him up, Bud acknowledged that his mother wakes him up most of the time, prompting Minuchin to respond, "So, she's your alarm clock" (pp. 43, 44).

Minuchin created the interpretive metaphor, MOTHER IS AN ALARM CLOCK, to identify the metaphoric structure of reality of the mother-son dyadic sub-system.

CASE EXAMPLE # 3: MOTHER IS THE FAMILY'S MEMORY BANK

Later in the session described above, Minuchin sought to make contact with Bud's father. When Minuchin asked Father when he gets up, Father replied, "Quarter to five, five o'clock" while looking at his wife who nodded, indicating her agreement. At this point, Minuchin asked whether Mother was the memory bank in the family, noting that both Bud and Father looked at mother for information. He suggested that Mother was a very busy person; "She is an alarm clock and a memory bank" (p. 45).

Minuchin created the metaphor MOTHER IS A MEMORY BANK to identify the family's metaphorically structured reality emphasizing Mother's role in the family system. Note that the data Minuchin used to create the metaphor were based on Minuchin's observation of the family's nonverbal, behavioral interaction in the session.

CASE EXAMPLE # 4: MOTHER IS WIRED TO THE FAMILY

Still later in the same session, Minuchin asked Bud a question and noted again that Mother nodded in agreement when Bud answered. Minuchin responded, "You know, she's wired to you people. [*To Mother*] Are you so wired that if he [Bud] answers, you say it?" (p. 47)

Minuchin explains that the "wiring" metaphor is not one that he normally uses; he selected it because it relates to the father's job as a foreman in an electronics shop. This illustrates one of Minuchin's favorite methods for creating a metaphoric interpretation of family structure using something concrete (i.e., wiring associated with electronics). His purpose is to accommodate to the family's frame of reference.

Minuchin's therapeutic objective, to identify and communicate the family structure by creating an interpretive metaphor that accommodates the family's unique frame of reference, is consistent with Metaphor Therapy's view that metaphors should reflect the client's—not a theory's— metaphoric structure of reality. The Structural Family Therapy approach differs from the explore/transform method in that the former is therapist-generated. It would seem that additional information regarding the metaphoric structure of family reality could be gained if the therapist attended to the family members' metaphoric language.

It is important to note, however, that the family system represents a different level of structured reality compared to the structured reality of its members. The concept of a family system is, *a priori*, interactive. It follows that a therapist seeking to identify and change a family's metaphoric structure of reality would rely heavily on observed behavioral interactive patterns among family members. This is also the case in Strategic Family Therapy discussed below, though, as we shall see, the interventions used in Strategic Family Therapy focus on direct methods of affecting the behavioral patterns of family members, in contrast with Structural Family Therapy's emphasis on formulating linguistic, metaphoric interventions.

METAPHOR THERAPY AND STRATEGIC FAMILY THERAPY

The Metaphoric Structure of Family Reality: Contributions of Strategic Family Therapy

Haley (1978) and Madanes (1981, 1984) are the major proponents of Strategic Family Therapy. Strategic Family Therapy holds that the essence of an interchange between family members lies in the metaphoric, in contrast to logical, characteristics of the communication.

Haley (1978) makes a distinction between digital (logical) and metaphoric communication. He defines digital communication as "that class of messages where each statement has a specific referent and only one referent. Something happens or does not happen–there is one stimulus and one response" (p. 83). Haley maintains that metaphoric communication is analogic in contrast to digital. In analogic communication, each message has multiple referents and deals with resemblances of one thing to another.* Further, each message refers to a context for other messages, "framing" the meaning of these other messages.

To illustrate the distinction between digital and analogic communication, Haley (1978) uses the example of a halftone newspaper photograph, noting that, although composed of a series of dots or "bits" of information, the newspaper picture is more than the sum total of the dots that make up the picture. "If we build such a picture by adding dots, they continue to be dots until a certain point at which the picture becomes recognizable as a representation of something" (pp. 84, 85). The change from digital to analogic communication occurs at the moment when the shift is made from dots (bits) to scene.

Note that the shift from digital to analogic communication involves a shift from dot to picture, from part to pattern. What is represented (re-presented) is an *image* of something else.

Haley emphasizes that metaphoric communication may be expressed either verbally or through action. Metaphoric communication expressed through action shows how something is metaphoric for something else by acting it out.

Haley's distinction differs somewhat from the one made earlier in Chapter 5. It was suggested that, in addition to distinguishing between metaphoric and logical (digital) cognition and communication, it is important to make a further distinction between imaginal cognition, which is associated with analogical thought, and metaphoric cognition, which combines both the analogical processes of imaginal cognition and the logical processes of propositional/syllogistic (digital) cognition. Thus, while Metaphor Therapy differs from Haley's view in that the former regards metaphor as integrating both logical and analogical cognitive processes, both approaches emphasize metaphoric in contrast to logical communication.

Strategic and Metaphor Therapy approaches also agree that communication has many metaphoric contexts. In Metaphor Therapy, however, some of these metaphoric contexts are *intrapersonal,* such as the metaphorms that make up the metaphoric structure of individual

---

*Clinical applications of the concepts described here are illustrated below.

reality of each family member, expressed in metaphoric language and early memory metaphors. Other metaphoric contexts may be *interpersonal*, such as (1) the current and past family patterns of interaction and communication emphasized by Structural and Strategic Family Therapy, (2) the sociocultural metaphoric contexts described by Lackoff and Johnson (1980), or (3) the transcultural metaphoric contexts represented in archetypes and myth. Any of these contexts may exert a causal influence on subjective meaning, behavior, or interpersonal communication.

Metaphor Therapy is an integrative approach in which changing the *interpersonal* family context is an important and effective way to change behavior and communication, and stimulating changes in *intrapersonal* (or, potentially, social and transcultural) metaphoric contexts can also produce these changes.

Ironically, to suggest that changing the interactive family context is the only way to change behavior of a family member would be reductionistic because it implies that the only (or primary) causal variables (metaphoric context) affecting a person's behavior exist at the level of the family system. This view is often found in the family therapy literature, however. For example, Haley (1978) states that "It would seem evident that insofar as the patient's communication is adaptive to his context, then the context must be changed for his communication to change" (p. 89), and adds that the patient's style can be changed only by "making organizational changes in the situation to which he is adapting" (p. 90).

In contrast, Metaphor Therapy maintains that the behavior and communication of each family member are adaptive to both intrapersonal and interpersonal contexts simultaneously. Thus, a therapist might change a family member's behavior (and, potentially the interactive patterns of that person's family) in individual therapy aimed at stimulating change in the family member's intrapersonal metaphoric context (metaphoric structure of individual reality).

Behavior as Metaphor in the Family System

Madanes (1981) suggests that all human behavior can be either analogical or metaphoric. A behavior is analogical to another behavior when one resembles the other in some way, even though they may be different in other respects. In contrast, "A behavior is metaphorical for another behavior when it symbolizes or is used in place of another behavior" (p. 225).

Recall that in Metaphor Therapy metaphoric structure refers to a "nonlinear" or "analogical" correspondence of pattern and organization between two things that are different when considered as discrete entities belonging to two different classes. Thus, spoken metaphors express metaphoric structure in language, and cognitive metaphors represent metaphoric structure in thought. Strategic Family Therapy adds a third dimension: behavioral metaphors, which express metaphoric structure in interpersonal family systems.

Symptoms as Metaphor in the Family System: Five Levels

According to Strategic Family Therapy, symptoms can be understood as metaphors about family life. For example, a wife with a physical pain in the neck that has no organic cause can be expressing metaphorically her opinion of some family members, e.g., "My husband's a pain in the neck." This view is similar to the psychodynamic concept of "organ jargon" (Adler, 1956) discussed earlier. Organ jargon was illustrated in the case of a woman with a skin rash that improved after the psychoanalytic therapist offered the interpretive metaphor, "She really gets under your skin, doesn't she," referring to the "irritation" and anger the client felt toward her sister and toward her mother.

Madanes (1981) suggests five ways in which a person's symptomatic behavior may be considered metaphoric:

1. A symptom may be a metaphor for an internal state, e.g., a headache may express a person's experience of more than one kind of pain.

2. A symptom may be a metaphor for another person's symptoms or internal states.* For example, if a child is afraid of and refuses to go to school, the child's fear may be metaphorical in that the child's fear may symbolize or represent the mother's fear concerning the child.

---

*Madanes introduces an interesting conceptual distinction. A symptom is viewed as analogical when it is similar to another family member's symptom, and an interaction between two or more family members is viewed as analogical when it is similar to the interaction between or among other family members. A symptom or interaction is considered metaphorical when it symbolizes and replaces another family member's symptom or the interaction between or among other family members.

3. The interaction between two people in a family can be a metaphor for the interaction between another dyad in the family. For example, a husband comes home upset and worried and his wife tries to reassure and comfort him. If their child develops a recurrent pain, "the father may come home and try to reassure and comfort the child in the same way that the wife was previously reassuring and comforting [the father]" (p. 226). The father's helpful involvement with the son precludes the father's helpless involvement with the wife, at least during the time in which the father is involved with the son. The interaction between father and son is metaphoric for the interaction between husband and wife because the former replaces the latter.

4. "The system of interaction around a symptom in one family member can be a metaphor for and replace another system of interaction around another issue in the family" (p. 226). For example, mother, father, and siblings may helpfully focus on a child's problem the way they focused on the father's problem before the child's problem developed. The new system of interaction focusing on the child's problem replaces the former system of interaction that focused on the father's problem.

5. "There may be a cyclical variation in the focus of interaction in families—sometimes centered on a symptomatic child, sometimes on the problem of a parent or on a marital difficulty" (p. 226). If the interactive pattern remains the same across these variations, (e.g., each involves helplessness and incongruity), then each variation is metaphoric for the other variations because each symbolizes and replaces the others.

It is interesting to note that Madanes' description implies a hierarchy of levels of metaphoric relationship (pattern/structure). Her first point pertains to an intrapersonal level of metaphoric relationship in that a symptom can be a metaphor for one or more states within the person. Point 2 identifies an interpersonal level of metaphoric relationship between two people. The same symptom mentioned in point 1 above may *also* be a metaphor for the internal image, belief, thought, or feeling of another family member. Point 3 identifies an interpersonal metaphoric relationship between two dyads, whereas point 4 refers to an interpersonal metaphoric relationship among two family subsystems involving three (triadic) or more individuals. Finally, point 5 introduces a metaphoric relationship of a different order. In Madanes' description of "cyclical variation," the interactive family pattern shifts focus *over time*. For example, at one time the focus of interaction may revolve around a symptomatic child, at another time the focus is different, e.g., focusing on the problem of a parent or on a marital problem. This is referred to as a *first-order change* (Watzlawick, Weakland, & Fisch, 1974), akin to changing the speed of a car by depressing the gas pedal.

It is noted, however, that, although the temporal focus of the interactive pattern changes, each interactive sequence resembles the other interactive sequences. For example, although the interactive sequences in a family may change focus among the child, the parent, and the marriage, all interactive sequences will share a similar pattern, e.g., all will involve helplessness and incongruity. This might be called second-order resemblance or "the pattern that connects" (Bateson, 1979). Therapeutic change at this level would involve a *second-order change* (Watzlawick et al., 1974), akin to changing the speed of a car by shifting from first to second gear.

12

Metaphor Therapy: Integrating Individual and Family Therapy

SYMPTOMS AS INTRA/INTERPERSONAL METAPHORIC STRUCTURES

Metaphor Therapy's view of symptoms integrates the perspectives of individual and family systems. The individual perspective focuses on the symptom as a metaphor for intrapersonal (intrapsychic) structures and processes, i.e., the metaphoric structure of individual reality.

Although both Madanes (1981) and Minuchin (Minuchin & Fishman, 1981) mention the individual, family systems therapy emphasizes the symptom as a metaphor for family members and/or family interactive patterns (Madanes, 1981). From the family systems perspective, a person develops a physical symptom for the purpose of communicating a metaphoric message to others through the language of bodily symptoms.

From the perspective of Metaphor Therapy and the principle that both individual and family reality are structured metaphorically, individual and family systems perspectives are different yet compatible approaches to understanding and treating symptoms as metaphor. Metaphor Therapy's goals and interventions draw on metaphoric methods from both individual and family systems models. Symptom change can result from changes in intrapersonal and/or interpersonal metaphoric structures. If metaphor is considered to include intrapersonal as well as interpersonal contexts, then Haley's comment that "When symptoms are seen as metaphors, the question is whether the metaphor has changed" (Haley, 1978, p. 97) can apply to both individual and family therapy.

TOWARD AN INTEGRATIVE METAPHOR THERAPY: A HOLOGRAPHIC-METAPHORIC MODEL

This section explores the hypothesis that intrapersonal and interpersonal metaphoric structures of reality may be *reciprocal*, based on the analogy that the family is like a hologram.

In a visual hologram, the information from the object becomes distributed over the surface of the photographic film (Pribram, 1985), so that "each small part of the hologram contains information from the entire original image and therefore can reproduce it" (Pribram, 1971, p. 150). This adds an additional dimension to the meaning of wholeness or holism, usually defined in terms of the whole being more than the sum of its parts. In the holographic analogy, holism means "the whole is encoded in each of the parts, and each of the parts can generate the whole."

When we examine the origin of the term "holism," however, the difference between viewing the whole as more than the sum of its parts and viewing the whole as encoded in each of its parts is not as great as it first appears. In fact, the original concept of holism, introduced in 1926 by Jan Smuts in his book, *Holism and Evolution,* includes both meanings! Smuts (1926/1961) proposes that the fundamental holistic character of a plant or animal is the unity of its parts such that the whole is more than the sum of its parts. He argues that this synthesis of parts within the whole gives a particular conformation or structure to the parts and alters their functions so that they function towards the whole. Thus, the whole and the parts reciprocally influence and determine each other so that "the whole is in the parts and the parts are in the whole, and this synthesis of whole and parts is reflected in the holistic character of the functions of the parts as well as of the whole" (p. xii).

Within the framework of Metaphor Therapy, the principle of reciprocal holism may be stated as follows: The metaphoric structure of family reality is in each family member's metaphoric structure of individual reality, and, each family member's metaphoric structure of individual reality is in the family's metaphoric structure of reality.

Minuchin's (Minuchin & Fishman, 1981) view seems consistent with this holographic-metaphoric perspective. Minuchin uses the term "holon" (Koestler, 1979) to refer to the individual, the nuclear family, the extended family, and the community. He maintains that each holon is both a whole and a part; each whole contains the part, and each part also contains the "program" that the whole imposes. Thus, "Part and whole contain each other in a continuing current, and ongoing process of communication and interrelationship" (p. 13). Minuchin also notes that, for the family and its members, "The actions and transactions of each one of the family members are not independent entities but part of a necessary movement in the choreography of a ballet. The movement of the whole needs four constrained dancers" (Minuchin & Fishman, 1981, p. 192).

Minuchin's metaphor, THE FAMILY IS A BALLET, suggests that (1) the movement in the ballet *as a whole* is mirrored in each of the roles and movements of the four dancers, and (2) the story of the ballet may be generated by an understanding of the movements of any of the four dancers, since each moves in relation to the others and in relation to the whole. This implies a multilevel "embedded systems" model where the metaphoric structure of individual reality of each family member is reflected in the metaphoric structure of family reality, and vice versa.

TOWARD AN INTEGRATIVE METAPHOR THERAPY:
A CASE EXAMPLE

This integrative approach could be applied in the case example discussed above, in which Minuchin identified the family's metaphoric structure by introducing the metaphor, THE FAMILY IS A TRAP. A therapist proceeding according to Metaphor Therapy's holographic-integrative framework would attend to, explore, and transform the metaphoric language of relevant family members, e.g., Mother and Father. For example, when Father says, "*it builds up* and *I hold it in* until *something will trigger it*," the therapist could invite Father to explore and transform this metaphoric image, thus helping Father to elaborate his (Father's) metaphoric structure of individual reality. Each family member could be asked if they agree with the metaphor "the family is a trap." Those who agree could be encouraged to take a moment and create an image of the family as a trap. The images could then be explored and compared, noting points of conflict and compatibility. Each family member could then be invited to transform his or her images. Those family members who did not agree with "the family is a trap" metaphor could be invited to create, explore, and ultimately transform their own metaphor for the family.*

SUMMARY AND CONCLUSIONS

The following conclusions can be drawn from the preceding discussion of current psychotherapies (Chapters 6-11) from the perspective of Metaphor Therapy:

1. Psychodynamic metaphoric methods that change a client's intrapersonal metaphoric context associated with the client's metaphoric structure of individual reality can also lead to changes in interpersonal and situational contexts in which the client is embedded.

2. Our personal mythic reality (metaphoric structure of individual reality) is revealed in our early memory metaphors. Understanding personal and transcultural myths may help

---

*I would like to thank Frances Willson, Ph.D., for her suggestions regarding these interventions.

us see both the universal and the unique in others. This understanding may, in turn, help us to embrace the similarities that connect and unify us within the family of humankind while helping us to appreciate the differences that make us unique.

3. Metaphor Therapy, because it incorporates and integrates both logical and imaginal cognition, contributes to an expanded "3-dimensional" view of cognition within which current models of therapy may be integrated.

4. Metaphor Therapy is suggested as a framework within which psychodynamic concepts and methods [that emphasize unconscious processes expressed symbolically through sensory-affective imagery (i.e., imaginal and metaphoric cognition)] are regarded as different yet compatible with Cognitive-Behavior Therapy concepts and methods [that emphasize cognitive processes expressed in self-talk, cognitive schemas, and beliefs (i.e., logical, syllogistic/propositional cognition)].

5. Some of the cases presented in Part I suggest that interpersonal (family) contextual patterns can change as a result of exploration and transformation of client metaphors and early memory metaphors, both of which represent intrapersonal metaphoric contexts associated with one's metaphoric structure of individual reality.

6. Strategic and Structural approaches to family systems therapy offer metaphoric interventions that differ from intrapersonal approaches in that they identify and seek to change interpersonal and situational metaphoric contexts in which individuals interact and to which they adapt. These interpersonal and situational metaphoric contexts reflect the metaphoric structure of family reality. Structural and Strategic family therapies offer unique, powerful concepts and interventions that suggest that the metaphoric structure of individual and family reality are variants of the metaphoric structure of reality.

7. The holographic-metaphoric model of the family proposes a reciprocal holism in which the metaphoric structure of family reality is in each family member's metaphoric structure of individual reality, and vice versa.

8. Metaphor Therapy offers a coherent framework within which both individual-intrapersonal and family-interpersonal metaphoric structures and interventions may be integrated.

13

Metaphor in Mind and Brain: Speculations on the Neuropsychology of Metaphor Therapy and Therapeutic Change

Working with our clients' creative imagination in Metaphor Therapy invites a curiosity concerning the brain's role in Metaphor Therapy and therapeutic change. This chapter presents an initial exploration of the possible connections between metaphoric processes in psychotherapy and certain aspects of neuropsychology. The following discussion will be limited to two areas: left and right hemisphere brain processes and Pribram's holographic model of the brain. Specifically, the ways in which hemispheric and holographic processes in the brain may mediate the therapeutic changes associated with exploring and transforming metaphoric language and early memory metaphors in therapy are explored. Potential research strategies for testing some of these relationships are suggested.

THE COGNITIVE REVOLUTION

It is important to state at the outset that I am not seeking to identify neuropsychological mechanisms that "cause" metaphoric cognition and language. Due largely to what is referred to as the *cognitive revolution* (see, for example, Bruner, 1990; Gardner, 1985; Hunt, 1989), reductionistic and deterministic causal models have given way to *interactive causal models* (Sperry, 1993).

For example, the assumption that feelings, beliefs, values, and behaviors are caused solely by biological factors illustrates what is now referred to as *biological reductionism*, because it assumes that these human phenomena can be explained by reducing them to their "underlying" biological components. In contrast, an explanation based on an interactive causal model maintains that "higher-order" factors such as thoughts, cognitions, and cultural values may also exert a causal influence on one's feelings, beliefs, values, and behaviors, and that these higher-order factors cannot be reduced to biological variables.

Bruner (1990) notes that the cognitive revolution sought to establish meaning as the central concept of psychology. According to Bruner, the aim of the cognitive revolution was to understand the "symbolic activities that human beings employed in constructing and in making sense not only of the world, but of themselves" (p. 2). The linguistic and cognitive metaphoric processes and structures of Metaphor Therapy are prime examples of such symbolic, meaning-making processes. They are also examples of the higher-order factors referred to by Sperry (1993) as "dynamic emergent properties of brain [processes and] states" that exert a causal influence on behavior (p. 880).

The cases described in Part I of this book suggest that metaphorms and the metaphoric structure of reality are subjective, mental structures that, when changed (transformed), can cause changes in beliefs, behavior, feelings, and interpersonal relationships. The possibility that these changes are mediated by neuropsychological brain processes will be explored next.

TOWARD A NEUROPSYCHOLOGY OF METAPHOR: AN INTERHEMISPHERIC PERSPECTIVE

Research on hemispheric asymmetry is often controversial and experimental results are sometimes contradictory (Hellige, 1993). Nevertheless, some lines of empirical research have yielded firmly established results based on converging data from a variety of research methods (Hellige, 1993). The following review is intended to be illustrative rather than exhaustive, and focuses on research findings for which there is considerable support.

The Division of Labor in the Brain: What's Left and What's Right

A substantial body of research on hemispheric asymmetry (see, for example, reviews by Hellige, 1993; Springer & Deutsch, 1989; Segalowitz, 1983) suggests that, for right-handed persons, the right hemisphere is superior to the left for processing the global aspects of the visual world (e.g., the outer contour of a face), as well as for the holistic, instantaneous processing of information. For these right-handed persons, however, the left hemisphere is superior to the right for most aspects of linguistic processing, such as overt speech, phonetic coding, syntactic and semantic processing, and analytic, sequential processing of information. In the normal brain, both hemispheres are necessary and function in a complementary way in many tasks, such as understanding language.

Toward a Neuropsychology of Metaphor

Comprehending Metaphor: A Right-Hemisphere Hypothesis. Recent reviews (Brownell, Simpson, Bihrle, Potter, & Gardner, 1990; Hough, 1990; Kaplan, Brownell, Jacobs, & Gardner, 1990) show that right-

hemisphere injury is more likely than left-hemisphere injury to produce difficulties in comprehending metaphors (Hellige, 1993). When
asked to select a picture that matched the metaphorical sentence "Sometimes you have to give someone a hand," for example, patients with
damage to their right hemisphere chose the drawing of somebody
offering someone a hand on a tray (Kosslyn & Koenig, 1992; Winner
& Gardner, 1977).*

  Generating Metaphoric Speech: An Interhemispheric Hypothesis. The picture that emerges from the above research suggests that the right hemisphere is the neurological locus for the content of a metaphor (Danesi,
1989). The task of *creating* metaphors, particularly novel metaphors,
would appear to involve both right and left hemispheres, however. In
the expression and elicitation of metaphor, the content (imagery) of
the metaphor appears to be processed in the right hemisphere, and
the structure or form (as a word uttered as part of verbal discourse) of
the metaphor appears to be processed in the left hemisphere (Danesi,
1989). Support for this hypothesis includes studies that show subjects
typically make a link between sensory/perceptual experience and
metaphoric statements (Malgady & Johnson, 1976; Verbrugge &
McCarrel, 1977; Verbrugge, 1980).

  Further, images have been shown to be a vehicle for relaying verbal metaphorical content (Pavio, 1979; Pavio & Clarke, 1986), and
subjects will typically report experiencing vivid images in reaction to
metaphors (Harris, Lakey & Marsalek, 1980). However, since metaphors must ultimately be coded conceptually and abstractly in order
to understand their meaning (a process for which the left hemisphere
is dominant) (see, for example, Riechmann & Coste, 1980), the comprehension and generation of novel metaphors would appear to involve both right and left hemispheres.

  The interhemispheric model posits a right hemisphere locus for the
more imaginative components of metaphor based on sensorial or
bodily experiences, and a left hemisphere locus for the transformation of such components into abstract principles of semantic organization (Danesi, 1989). Danesi (1989) suggests that the "neurological flow"
accompanying the creation of novel metaphors is likely to go from

---

*Persons with schizophrenia also tend to interpret metaphoric expressions concretely. For
example, as an intern I observed an intake interview with a woman with schizophrenia who
had been admitted to the inpatient psychiatric ward. The psychologist began the session by
asking, "What brought you to the hospital?" She responded, "A '57 Blue Chevy."

content (the right hemisphere) to form (the left hemisphere), although she notes that this hypothesis would have to be tested experimentally. Because the exploration and transformation of linguistic and early memory metaphors involve the creation of novel imagery that is subsequently communicated in words, these Metaphor Therapy interventions may also flow from the right hemisphere to the left. Possible procedures for testing this hypothesis are discussed below.

Summary

Metaphor stands with a foot in each hemisphere. The analytic, sequential, left hemisphere is particularly well-suited for syllogistic/ propositional/logical cognition, while the global-visuospatial, holistic right hemisphere is particularly well-suited for processing imaginal cognition. Metaphoric cognition unites both imaginal and syllogistic cognition and may also employ the complementary functions of both hemispheres of the brain. Although most complex tasks involve complementary abilities of both hemispheres (Hellige, 1993), metaphor appears to be unique as a verbal utterance whose creation requires both right and left hemispheric processes.

Hemispheric Asymmetry, Metaphor Therapy, and Therapeutic Change

When a metaphor is conceived in thought and introduced in verbal communication, the metaphor-maker attends primarily to the external situation (the topic of the metaphor) in contrast to the internal metaphoric image (the vehicle of the metaphor). We may posit that linear, verbal, logical linguistic and cognitive processes are primary when attention is focused on the situation, and that left hemisphere processes are also primary.

When the client enters and explores the metaphoric image, the linguistic and cognitive emphasis shifts from the topic, i.e., the life situation to which the metaphor refers, to the image (vehicle) conveyed in the metaphor. Imaginal linguistic and cognitive processes have now moved from the background to center stage. We may posit that a shift in the relative activation of left and right hemisphere processing occurs as a client enters the domain of the metaphoric imagination: left hemisphere activity is dominant prior to entering into the metaphoric image, whereas right hemisphere activity is dominant after the client has entered into and begins to explore the metaphoric image.

Exploring and transforming metaphoric imagery involve both imagistic and verbal-linguistic processes. Once the client enters the metaphoric image and remains engaged in exploring the image, sensory images emerge and are then described and communicated verbally. What seems crucial is that the activity of exploring and transforming a metaphor starts with a sensory image that is subsequently communicated through language. Other factors such as the close link between emotions and imagery and the right hemisphere offer additional support for this view. These factors are discussed below.

Although most of the research on hemispheric asymmetry appears to support the hypothesis that right hemisphere activity is greater than left hemisphere activity during the exploration and transformation of metaphoric imagery, some studies suggest a different view. For example, one line of research is consistent with the hypothesis that the generation of mental images from memory is generally a function of the *left* hemisphere (Hellige, 1993). Studies of brain-damaged patients (Farah, 1984; Farah, Levine, & Calvanio, 1988), split-brain patients (Farah et al., 1985; Kosslyn et al., 1985), and normal subjects (Farah, 1986; Kosslyn, 1988) all implicate the left hemisphere in the generation of mental images under most circumstances (Farah, Weisberg, & Monheit, 1989). These studies suggest that the left hemisphere could also play an active role in the exploration and transformation of metaphoric imagery.

Future research must address the fact that the stimuli used in hemispheric asymmetry studies is usually far removed from the clinical situation in which clients create and explore their metaphors. For example, emotional and contextual factors influencing the mental images generated by a client while exploring a metaphoric image (including those associated with the creation of the original metaphor) typically play no role in the hemispheric asymmetry research, including research on the generation of mental imagery mentioned above.

The goal of this discussion is to generate hypotheses that may guide future research on hemispheric asymmetry and psychotherapy. For example, by using techniques such as the electroencephalographic

(EEG) and lateral eye movements (LEMs)* to measure localized brain activity, the relative activation of left and right hemispheres could be measured directly during a psychotherapy session. Initial readings would offer a base line for comparing relative brain activity when metaphors are generated, explored, transformed, and subsequently related back to the client's life issue. At present, it appears that the process of exploring and transforming metaphoric images is an inter-hemispheric process. Future research may help clarify the ways each hemisphere contributes to this process.

The Role of the Right Hemisphere in Human Emotion

Studies with both brain-injured patients and neurologically normal individuals suggest that the right hemisphere is dominant for the per-ception of emotion (Borod et al., 1990; Bowers, Bauer, Coslett, & Heilman, 1985; Bryden, 1982; Hellige, 1993; Levy, Heller, Banich, & Burton, 1983), for identifying emotional tone of spoken material (Ley & Bryden, 1982; Bryden & MacRae, 1989), and for recognizing and producing affective components or language (Ross, 1981; Ross & Meuslam, 1979). Other research has shown that the right hemisphere is superior to the left hemisphere in the expression of emotion (Borod & Caron, 1980; Campbell, 1978; Chaurasia & Goswami, 1975; Heller & Levy, 1981; Kolb & Taylor, 1981; Tucker, Watson, & Heilman, 1977), and in the forming of such unconscious mental processes as unac-countable emotion (Kostandov & Arzumanov, 1986).

Another line of research suggests that the right hemisphere is domi-nant for negative emotions and the left hemisphere is dominant for positive emotions in adults (Davidson, 1992; Davidson et al., 1979; d'Elia & Perris, 1973, 1974; Ketterer, 1982; Meyers & Smith, 1987; Perris, 1974, 1975) and in infants and children (Davidson, 1988, 1992; Fox, 1991). However, Gainotti, Caltagirone, and Zoccolotti (1993) note that much of the clinical and experimental data (e.g., Borod, Koff, Perlman-Lorch, & Nicholas, 1986; Bowers, Bauer, Coslett, & Heilman,

---

* Silberman and Weingartner (1986) note that the relationship between LEMs and lateral hemispheric activation must be considered hypothetical at present (see review by Ehrlichman & Weinberger, 1978). Thus, future research should employ multiple measures of hemispheric asymmetry.

1985; Duda & Brown, 1984; Etcoff, 1984; Gage & Safer, 1985; Hirschman & Safer, 1982; Ladavas, Umilta, & Ricci-Bitti, 1980; Strauss & Kaplan, 1980; Strauss & Moscovitch, 1981; Suberi & McKeever, 1979; Wylie & Goodale, 1988) have failed to confirm the hypothesis of the right hemisphere for negative emotions and of specialization of the left hemisphere for positive emotions.

At least one study (Ferguson, 1989) failed to support the concept of an asymmetric affective bias for the two hemispheres when the stimuli were words in contrast to the more typical nonverbal stimuli, such as tones, cartoon films, or pictures of faces.

The convergence of many lines of research using diverse methodologies applied to a wide variety of clinical and normal populations constitutes "strong evidence that there are emotion-related processes which take place asymmetrically in the brain" (Silberman & Weingartner, 1986, p. 342). These findings are most consistent with the hypothesis that the exploration and transformation of emotionally charged metaphoric imagery utilizes mainly right hemisphere processes, especially when the emotional affect is negative. Furthermore, if the left hemisphere is dominant for positive emotions as some studies suggest, then left hemisphere activation might be expected to increase (and right hemisphere activity to decrease) at the point where clients transform their "negative" metaphoric image (a tunnel) into a "positive" metaphoric image (a derailer). These hypotheses suggest directions for further research.

Hemispheric Asymmetry, Metaphorms and the Metaphoric Structure of Reality

Metaphoric structure was defined earlier as a "non-linear" correspondence of pattern and organization between two things that are different when considered as discrete entities belonging to two different "linear" logical classes (see Chapter 5). It was also suggested that spoken metaphors express metaphoric structure in language, while cognitive metaphors represent metaphoric structure in thought. The global, synthetic, holistic qualities of the right hemisphere seem well suited to performing the neurological brain functions associated with non-linear correspondence of pattern and organization between two things, while the sequential, analytic, verbal qualities of the left hemisphere seem well suited to performing the neurological brain functions associated with the correspondence of two things that are different when considered as discrete entities belonging to two different linear, logical classes.

In summary, it appears that metaphor, metaphoric structure, metaphorms, and the metaphoric structure of reality involve complementary processes at linguistic, cognitive, and neurological levels. However, even if it were to be shown that the brain functions described here are not morphologically related to or located exclusively in specific hemispheres, the thesis advanced here regarding the functional relations of these processes should still hold.

We now turn our attention to exploring possible relationships between Metaphor Therapy and holographic processes in the brain.

THE POWER OF METAPHOR THERAPY: A HOLOGRAPHIC HYPOTHESIS

This section begins with a discussion of how Pribram developed his theory of the holographic brain in order to account for key aspects of memory and image formation. Implications of the holographic brain theory are discussed in relation to Metaphor Therapy and therapeutic change.

Memory, Imagery, and Holographic Processes in the Brain

Proposing the existence of neural holographic processes offers a compelling explanation of certain brain functions, especially memory and imagery formation (Pribram, 1985).

In the late 1940's, Dennis Gabor developed an efficient way of storing images of objects by transforming the light patterns emanating from the object into wave patterns and then storing these wave patterns on a photographic plate. Gabor named the stored wave pattern a *hologram* because the information from the object becomes distributed over the surface of the photographic film (Pribram, 1985). Thus, "each small part of the hologram contains information from the entire original image and therefore can reproduce it" (Pribram, 1971, p. 150).

Pribram notes that the hologram has a fantastic capacity to store information. Many different patterns can be simultaneously stored on a holographic plate–some 10 billion bits of information have been usefully stored holographically in a cubic centimeter! He concludes that, "For the problems of [human] perception, especially image formation and the fantastic capacity of recognition memory, holographic* description has no peer" (Pribram, 1971, p. 152).

Inspired by the idea that the distributed memory store in the brain might resemble this holographic record, Pribram developed a theory based on known neuroanatomy and known neurophysiology that could account for the brain's distributed memory store in holographic terms. Subsequent research has supported the view that the auditory, somatosensory, motor, and visual systems of the brain process input from the senses in the wave pattern or frequency domain (Pribram, 1971, 1991).

Metaphor and Sensory Imagery: A Neurocognitive Hypothesis

The sensory modalities employed in sensory imagery include visual, auditory, tactile, gustatory, and olfactory senses (Gallup & Cameron, 1992).** I will use the term *holosensory imagery* to refer to the various modes of sensory imagery considered as a group. The concept of holosensory imagery suggests that whenever we think or speak using imaginal cognition and metaphoric cognition, we activate and utilize holographic neurological processes in the brain. As Pribram has shown, all of these modes of holosensory imagery are processed and stored as distributive wave (or frequency) patterns.

The Power of Metaphor Therapy: A Holographic Hypothesis

Metaphor Therapy emphasizes metaphoric interventions involving exploring and transforming metaphoric imagery originating with

---

*Pribam's recent work (1990, 1991) draws even more heavily on the work of Gabor. Pribram has renamed his theory "Holonomic Brain Theory," noting that "the term holonomic was chosen to distinguish it from holographic and still connote that it is 'holistic' and lawful" (Pribram, 1990). Pribram's revisions are designed to deal with various challenges to the theory involving levels of complexity and distinctions that are not relevant to the present discussion. It is important to note that Pribram's revised holonomic theory incorporates the holographic model (Pribram, 1994). I will continue to use the earlier *holographic* terminology because it conveys a better intuitive understanding of these rather abstract concepts. However, the reader should keep in mind that broader holonomic principles are at work at neurological levels.

**See Gallup and Cameron (1992) for a more extensive discussion of sensory modalities involved in metaphor.

either a client's metaphoric language or a client's metaphoric early recollections. As we have seen, interventions where clients explore and transform their spoken metaphors involve shifting attention to the sensory imagery created by clients to represent the situation to which the metaphor refers.

Pribram (1985) points out that our ears and acoustic nervous systems reconstruct the sound of a three-dimensional acoustic image from two speakers. The resulting sound is perceived in a location (e.g., the midpoint between the two speakers) we know to be incapable of producing that sound. Further, research on brain cells shows that both auditory and visual cells are frequency analyzers. Whereas cells in the auditory sensory modality analyze tone patterns in time, cells in the visual sense modality analyze visual patterns in space (Pribram, 1978).

Pribram concludes that the human experience of image formation in the mind's eye is explained by the fact that our visual nervous systems reconstruct three-dimensional holographic images that are projected away from their source of origin as wave or frequency patterns in the brain. This is consistent with Kosslyn's work on imagery discussed in Chapter 5, particularly with regard to the formation of the inner image at a site away from where the neuronal activity takes place (Kosslyn, 1980). Since this imaging process also characterizes the exploration and transformation of linguistic and early memory images, this explanation should also apply to these metaphoric interventions.

Pribram (1971) notes that retrieval from the more permanent memory store requires only the repetition of the pattern (or essential parts of the pattern) that originally initiated storage. Could this be what happens in the brain when early memory metaphors are used in therapy?

Recall that the procedure for eliciting early memory metaphors begins when clients are asked to form an image in their mind of a recent instance of a disturbing problem or situation. They are then asked to use as many sensory modalities as they can—to remember what they heard, saw, smelled, touched, or tasted. Clients are also asked to feel again in their body the feelings they had at the time of the recent event. When clients are asked to recollect the first sensory image from early childhood that comes to mind as they vividly image and affectively experience a recent troubling event, the current image, as a part pattern, may trigger the recall of a "more deeply embedded and permanently stored organizing pattern," i.e., the early recollection image. Put differently, the early recollection may be a metaphor for the current situation because the holographic sensory image construction of the perceived current experience is sufficiently close (isomorphic) to the deeply embedded, holographically stored organizing pattern of an early recollection image to cause the early recollection to be "read out" of the stored wave pattern.

These more permanent holograms may be the neurological analogues to such clinical concepts as (1) cognitive schema and deep structure in cognitive-behavior therapy (especially when formulated in imaginal-cognitive and metaphoric-cognitive modes in contrast to the propositional/logical cognitive mode); (2) the schema of apperception and the life style composed of images of self, life, others, and goal/ideal in Adlerian Psychology; (3) primary process images and screen memories in Psychoanalysis; and (4) archaic self-other representational images in object relations theory.

It is also interesting to consider what may occur when clients are invited to transform their early recollection. It was suggested earlier that, at linguistic and cognitive levels, the transformatory process occurs through the operation of conscious language and thought on the recollected childhood image. Could it be that the act of rewriting the early recollection narrative can sometimes result in a new (transformed) holographic (holosensory) image of the memory? Furthermore, might this transformed holographic image then be redistributed over a large surface of the brain?

Similar questions can be asked about spoken metaphors. The exploration and transformation of a spoken metaphor may transform the neural holographic metaphoric image, which, in turn, may be redistributed over a large surface area of the brain. The transformed image could cause a subsequent change in the neural organizational pattern. For example, when Carol (Introduction) transforms her metaphoric self-other image from a locomotive (her husband) and a tunnel (Carol) to a locomotive and a derailer, her transformed neural hologram may be immediately distributed over the same or a similar brain area covered by the original metaphoric image. This hypothesis has intuitive appeal because it appears consistent with the significant behavioral, attitudinal, and emotional changes that clients sometimes make in their problem situation (as Carol did in relation to her husband), even when no other intervention follows their transformation of the metaphor. Perhaps such changes are due, at least in part, to changes in holographically stored early memory images which, because they are distributed over large areas of the brain, stimulate changes in one's metaphoric structure of reality, leading to significant changes in one's beliefs, feelings, behaviors, and relationships.

Metaphorms as Neurological Holograms

Recall that the metaphoric structure of individual reality is comprised of metaphorms (metaphoric images) of self, others, and life, and metaphoric relational images of self-in-relation-to-self, self-in-relation-to-others, and self-in-relation-to-life. Further, metaphorms and the metaphoric structure of reality are represented in the metaphoric imagery of linguistic and early recollection metaphors. It follows that if metaphoric images are neural holograms and early recollections are stored and retrieved according to neurological holographic principles, then metaphorms and the metaphoric structure of individual reality are likewise constructed, stored, and retrieved according to neural holographic principles.

SUMMARY AND CONCLUSIONS

It appears that the creation of spontaneous spoken metaphors and early memory metaphors evokes sensory images that may engage neurological holographic processes that are distributed over large areas of the brain. A metaphoric image may create a resemblance, not merely between the image and the external referent situation, but between neural holographically encoded representations and the external situation (as perceived by the individual). These representations, in turn, may relate to primary memory patterns holographically encoded early in life. The power of metaphorical interventions may lie in the fact that metaphorical images are distributed throughout the brain in a holographic manner. If so, then exploring linguistic metaphors and early memory metaphors may activate this expansive network, and transforming metaphors may reverberate throughout the entire range of distribution of the image and/or memory.

Epilogue

The Pattern That Connects: Metaphoric Structure in Mind and Nature

It was one of those magical mornings on the Big Sur coast. As the fog melted under the warm sun, Gregory Bateson and Fritjof Capra sat on the deck outside the Esalen lodge. There, high above the surf and headlands, Bateson pondered the limitations of logic and the nature of living things. Capra (1988) recalls the conversation:

> "Logic is a very elegant tool," [*Bateson*] said, "and we've got a lot of mileage out of it for two thousand years or so. The trouble is, you know, when you apply it to crabs and porpoises, and butterflies and habit formation"—his voice trailed off, and he added after a pause, looking out over the ocean—"you know, to all those pretty things"—and now, looking straight at me—"logic won't quite do."
> "No?" [*Capra responded.*]
> "It won't do," [*Bateson*] continued animatedly, "because that whole fabric of living things is not put together by logic."...
> "So what do they use instead?"
> "Metaphor," Bateson replied, "that's how this whole fabric of mental interconnections holds together. Metaphor is right at the bottom of being alive." (pp. 76, 77)

Our first task in this Epilogue is to understand Bateson's view that metaphor is the principle by which the whole fabric of living things is put together. The key lies in Bateson's observation that metaphor is the pattern that connects, i.e., the pattern that defines the evolutionary relatedness of living things.

170

METAPHOR: THE LANGUAGE OF NATURE

As the title suggests, Bateson (1979) proposes in his extraordinary book, *Mind and Nature: A Necessary Unity*, that mind and nature are unified within a single principle, "the pattern that connects." Bateson maintains that *metaphor is the pattern that connects—a pattern that characterizes the evolution of all living organisms.*

Capra (1988) notes that "one of Bateson's main aims in his study of epistemology was to point out that logic was unsuitable for the description of biological patterns" (p. 80). To understand Bateson's reasoning and his identification of metaphor as the principle most suitable for the description of biological patterns, we must understand Bateson's distinction between first-order and second-order correspondence in nature.

The Metaphoric Structure of Biological Evolution

Bateson (1979) says that the reason he chose to be a biologist was to learn how "the total biological world in which we live and have our being" is put together (p. 8). Although this question had occupied him since he was a boy, it was not until the 1950's, while he was teaching a course at the California School of Fine Arts in San Francisco, that these ideas came into clear focus around a central question: "What is the pattern that connects all the living creatures?" (p. 8).

Bateson entered the classroom one evening carrying two brown paper bags, which he placed side by side on his desk. Taking a freshly cooked crab out of one bag and placing it on the desk, he asked his art students, "*How are you related to this creature? What pattern connects you to it?*" (p. 9).

The students looked at the crab. Their first observation was that it was *symmetrical*—the right side resembled the left.

Next, they observed that one claw was bigger than the other.

So it was *not* symmetrical!

Then somebody uttered what Bateson regarded as a "beautiful and noble statement: *'Yes, one claw is bigger than the other, but both claws are made of the same parts'*" (p. 9). The student had identified "the pattern that connects," i.e., the resemblance of relations, pattern, and organization between two things of different size.

Bateson had established his first point: the thing that characterizes living things is the *similar relationship* among parts within the organism. Next, he pointed out that the same was true for the students' bodies. The upper arm corresponds to the upper thigh, the wrist corresponds to the ankle, the fingers to the toes, etc. Anatomy is repetitive and rhythmical, Bateson noted.

Bateson had laid the groundwork. He reached into the other brown paper bag sitting on the desk before him, pulled out a cooked lobster, and said, "Let us call these patterns *within* the individual growing crab *first-order connections.* But now we look at crab and lobster and we again find connection by pattern. Call it *second-order connection,* or phylogenetic homology" (p. 10). Phylogenetic homology is defined as "A formal resemblance between two organisms such that the relations between certain parts of A are similar to the relations between corresponding parts of B. Such formal resemblance is considered to be evidence of evolutionary relatedness" (Bateson, 1979, p. 228).

METAPHOR: THE PATTERN THAT CONNECTS MIND AND NATURE

Note that this second-order "pattern that connects" the evolution of living things has the same structure noted earlier in the mental processes of metaphoric language and metaphoric cognition. Carol's metaphor, MY HUSBAND BARGES INTO THE HOUSE LIKE A LOCOMOTIVE, illustrated the fact that metaphoric language and cognition create a formal resemblance between two things such that the aspects of the relationship between Carol's husband and Carol were similar to the aspects of the relationship between a locomotive and a tunnel. Carol created a metaphor that identified the pattern that connects her and her husband.

It is clear from this analysis that Metaphor Therapy and the metaphoric structure of reality also rest on the principle of metaphor as the pattern that connects. This is consistent with Bateson's view that metaphor is the pattern that connects in the domain of mind and in the domain of nature. In fact, mind and nature are unified under this single principle.

It appears that long before humans spoke or thought in metaphor, and long before metaphor was the source of novelty in language and thought, nature spoke its own language of metaphor–the pattern that connects. Indeed, the metaphoric structure of reality in individuals, families, and within and across cultures may be seen as the expression in humankind of the metaphoric structure underlying the biological evolution of all living things.

References

Adler, A. (1956). *The individual psychology of Alfred Adler: A systematic presentation in selections from his writings*. H. & R. Ansbacher (Eds.). New York: Basic Books.

Aleksandrowicz, D. B. (1962). The meaning of metaphor. *Bulletin of the Menninger Clinic, 26,* 92–101.

Ansbacher, H. (1946). Adler's place in the psychology of memory. *Journal of Personality, 15,* 197–207.

Ansbacher, H. (1989). Adlerian psychotherapy: The tradition of brief psychotherapy. *Individual Psychology, 20* (nos. 1 and 2), 26–33.

Attneave, C. L. (1984). Themes striving for harmony: Conventional mental health services and American Indian traditions. In S. Sue & T. Moore (Eds.), *The pluralistic society: A community mental health perspective* (pp. 149–166). New York: Human Services Press.

Baker, H., & Baker, M. (1987). Heinz Kohut's Self Psychology: An overview. *American Journal of Psychiatry, 144:* 1, 1–8.

Barker, P. (1985). *Using metaphors in psychotherapy*. New York: Brunner/Mazel.

Baruth, L., & Eckstein, D. (1978). *Life style: Theory, practice, and research*. Dubuque, IA: Kendall/Hunt.

Bateson, G. (1979). *Mind and nature: A necessary unity*. New York: E. P. Dutton.

Beck, A. (1976). *Cognitive therapy and the emotional disorders*. New York: International Universities Press.

Beck, A., Rush, A., Shaw, B., & Emery, G. (1979). *Cognitive therapy of depression*. New York: Guilford Press.

Bettleheim, B. (1984). *Freud and man's soul*. New York: Vintage Books.

Bloom, B. (1981). Focused single-session therapy: Initial development and evaluation. In S. Budman (Ed.), *Forms of brief therapy* (pp. 167–216). New York: Guilford Press.

Borod, J. C., & Caron, H. (1980). Facedness and emotion related to lateral dominance, sex and expression type. *Neuropsychologia, 18,* 237–242.

Borod, J. C., Koff, E., Perlman-Lorch, M., & Nicholas, M. (1986). The expression and perception of facial emotion in brain-damaged patients. *Neuropsychologia, 24,* 169–180.

Borod, J. C., St. Clair, J., Koff, E., & Alpert, M. (1990). Perceiver and pose asymmetries in processing facial emotion. *Brain and Cognition, 13,* 167–177.

Bowers, D., Bauer, R. M., Coslett, H. B., & Heilman, K. M. (1985). Processing of face by patients with unilateral hemispheric lesions. I. Dissociations between judgements of facial affect and facial identity. *Brain and Cognition, 4,* 258–272.

Brenner, C. (1974). *An elementary textbook of psychoanalysis*. New York: Anchor Press.

Brewer, W. (1986). What is autobiographical memory? In D. C. Rubin (Ed.), *Autobiographical memory* (pp. 25–49). New York: Cambridge University Press.

Brownell, H. H., Simpson, T. L., Bihrle, A. M., Potter, H. H., & Gardner, H. (1990). Appreciation of metaphoric alternative word meanings by left and right brain-damaged patients. *Neuropsychologia, 28,* 375–384.

Bruner, J. (1990). *Acts of meaning*. Cambridge, MA.: Harvard University Press.

Bryden, M. P. (1982). *Laterality: Functional asymmetry in the intact brain*. New York: Academic Press.

Bryden, M. P., & MacRae, L. (1989). Dichotic laterality effects obtained with emotional words. *Neuropsychiatry, Neuropsychology, and Behavioral Neurology, 1,* 171–176.

Budman, S. (Ed.). (1981). *Forms of brief therapy*. New York: Guilford Press.

Campbell, J. (1986). *The inner reaches of outer space: Metaphor as myth and as religion.* New York: Harper & Row.

Campbell, R. (1978). Asymmetries in interpreting and expressing a posed facial expression. *Cortex, 14,* 327–342.

Capra, F. (1988). *Uncommon wisdom: Conversations with remarkable people.* New York: Simon and Schuster.

Chaurasia, B. D., & Goswami, H. K. (1975). Functional asymmetry in the face. *Acta Anat (Basel), 91,* 154–160.

Cohen, T. (1979). Metaphor and the cultivation of intimacy. In S. Sacks (Ed.), *On metaphor* (pp. 1–10). Chicago IL.: University of Chicago Press.

Cox, M., & Theilgaard, A. (1987). *Mutative metaphors in psychotherapy: The aeolian mode.* London: Tavistock.

Danesi, M. (1989). The neurological coordinates of metaphor. *Communication and Cognition, 22* (1), 73–86.

Davenloo, H. (Ed.), (1980). *Short-term dynamic psychotherapy.* New York: Jason Aronson.

Davidson, R. J. (1988). EEG measures of cerebral asymmetry: Conceptual and methodological issues. *International Journal of Neuroscience, 39,* 71–89.

Davidson, R. J. (1992). Emotion and affective style: Hemispheric substrates. *Psychological Science, 3,* 39–43.

Davidson R. J., Schwartz, G. E., Saron, C., Bennett, J., & Goleman, D. J. (1979). Frontal versus parietal EEG asymmetry during positive and negative affect. *Psychophysiology, 16,* 202–203.

DeCasper, A. J., & Fifer, W. P. (1980). Of human bonding: Newborns prefer their mothers' voices. *Science, 208,* 1174–1176.

d'Elia, G., & Perris, C. (1973). Cerebral functional dominance and depression: An analysis of EEG amplitude in depressed patients. *Acta Psychiatrica Scandinavica, 49,* 191–197.

d'Elia, G., & Perris, C. (1974). Cerebral functional dominance and memory functions: An analysis of EEG integrated amplitude in depressive psychotics. *Acta Psychiatrica Scandinavica, Supplement, 255,* 143–157.

Dreikurs, R. (1973). Private logic. In H. Mosak (Ed.), *Alfred Adler: His influence on psychology today* (pp. 19–32). New Jersey: Noyes Press.

Dreikurs, S. (1986). *Cows can be purple: My life and art therapy.* Chicago: Alfred Adler Institute.

Duda, P. D., & Brown, J. (1984). Lateral asymmetry of positive and negative emotions. *Cortex, 20,* 253–261.

Duhl, B. (1983). *From the inside out and other metaphors: Creative and integrative approaches to training in systems thinking.* New York: Brunner/Mazel.

Edelson, J. (1983). Freud's use of metaphor. *Psychoanalytic Study of the Child, 38,* 17–59.

Ehrlichman, H., & Weinberger, A. (1978). Lateral eye movements and hemispheric asymmetry: A critical review. *Psychological Bulletin, 85,* 1080–1101.

Ekstein, R. (1966). *Children of time and space, of action and impulse.* New York: Appleton-Century-Crofts.

Ellis, A. (1973). *Humanistic psychotherapy: The Rational-Emotive approach.* New York: McGraw-Hill.

Ellis A. (1989). Rational-Emotive Therapy. In R. Corsini (Ed.), *Current psychotherapies* (pp. 197–238). Itasca, IL: F. E. Peacock.

Etcoff, N. L. (1984). Perceptual and conceptual organization of facial emotions: Hemispheric differences. *Brain and Cognition, 3,* 385–412.

Evans, M. B. (1988). The role of metaphor in psychotherapy and personality change: A theoretical reformulation. *Psychotherapy, 25*(4), 543–551.

Fagan, J. (1973). Infants' delayed recognition memory and forgetting. *Journal of Experimental Child Psychology, 16,* 424–450.

Farah, M. J. (1984). The neurological basis of mental imagery: A componential analysis. *Cognition, 18,* 245–272.

Farah, M. J. (1986). The laterality of mental image generation: A test with normal subjects. *Neuropsychologia, 24,* 541–551.

Farah, M. J., Gazzaniga, M. S., Holtzman, J., & Kosslyn, S. (1985). A left hemisphere basis for mental imagery? *Neuropsychologia, 23,* 115–118.

Farah, M. J., Levine, D. N., & Calvanio, R. (1988). A case study of mental imagery deficit. *Brain and Cognition, 8,* 147–164.

Farah, M. J., Weisberg, L. L., & Monheit, M. (1989). Brain activity underlying mental imagery: Event-related potentials during mental image generation. *Journal of Cognitive Neuroscience, 1*(4), 302–316.

Ferguson, E. D., (1989). Motivational influences on word recognition: II. Affective coding. *Bulletin of the Psychonomic Society, 27*(4), 307–310.

Fox, N. A. (1991). If it's not left, it's right. *American Psychologist, 46,* 863–872.

Freud, S. (1950). Screen memories. In J. Strachey (Ed. and Trans.), *The standard edition of the complete psychological works of Sigmund Freud* (Vol. 5, pp. 47-69). London: Hogarth Press. (Original work published 1899).

Freud, S. (1923/1960). *The ego and the id* (J. Riviere, Trans., J. Strachey, Ed.). New York: W. W. Norton. (Original work published 1923).

Gage, D. F., and Safer, M. A. (1985). Hemisphere differences in the mood state-dependent effect for recognition of emotional faces. *Journal of Experimental Psychology: Learning, Memory and Cognition, 11,* 752–763.

Gainotti, G., Caltagirone, C., & Zoccolotti, P. (1993). Left/right and cortical/subcortical dichotomies in the neuropsychological study of human emotions. *Cognition and Emotion, 7*(1), 71–93.

Gallup, Jr., G., & Cameron, P. (1992). Modality specific metaphors: Is our mental machinery "colored" by a visual bias? *Metaphor and Symbolic Activity, 7*(2), 93–98.

Gardner, H. (1985). *The mind's new science: A history of the cognitive revolution.* New York: Basic Books.

Gendlin, E. T. (1981). *Focusing.* New York: Bantam Books.

Gold, L. (1978). Life-style and dreams. In L. Baruth & D. Eckstein (Eds.), *Life-style: Theory, practice, and research* (pp. 24–30). Dubuque, IA: Kendall/Hunt.

Gold, L. (1988). A contemporary view of dream interpretation and therapy. *Festschrift aus anlass der verleihung des Dr, Margrit Egner-Preises 1988 zum thema "der traum."* Zurich, Switzerland.

Gordon, D. (1978). *Therapeutic metaphors: Helping others through the looking glass.* Cupertino, CA: META Publications.

Greenberg, J. and Mitchell, S. (1983). *Object relations in psychoanalytic theory.* Cambridge, MA: Harvard University Press.

Haley, J. (1978). *Problem-solving therapy: New strategies for effective family therapy.* New York: Harper Colophon Books.

Hamilton, N. G. (1988). *Self and others: Object relations theory in Practice.* Northvale, NJ: Jason Aronson.

Harris, R. J., Lakey, M. A., & Marsalek, F. (1980). Metaphors and images: Rating, reporting, remembering. In R. R. Hoffman & R. P. Honeck (Eds.), *Cognition and figurative language* (pp. 231–258). Hillsdale, NJ: Erlbaum.

Heller, W., & Levy, J. (1981). Perception and expression of emotion in right-handers and left-handers. *Neuropsychologia, 19,* 263–272.

Hellige, J. B. (1993). *Hemispheric assymetry: What's right and what's left.* Cambridge, MA: Harvard University Press.

Hirschman, R. S., & Safer, M. A. (1982). Hemisphere differences in perceiving positive and negative emotions. *Cortex, 18,* 569–580.

Hough, M. S. (1990). Narrative comprehension in adults with right and left hemisphere brain-damage: Theme organization. *Brain and Language, 38*, 253–277.

Hunt, E. (1989). Cognitive science: Definition, status, and questions. *Annual Review of Psychology, 40*, 603–629.

Johnson-Laird, P. (1981). Mental models in cognitive science. In D. A. Norman (Ed.), *Perspectives on cognitive science* (pp. 147–191). Norwood, NJ: Ablex.

Jones, A. C. (1985). Psychological functioning in Black Americans: A conceptual guide for use in psychotherapy. *Psychotherapy, 22*, 363–369.

Kaplan, J. A., Brownell, H. H., Jacobs, J. R., & Gardner, H. (1990). The effects of right hemisphere damage on the pragmatic interpretation of conversational remarks. *Brain and Language, 38*, 315–333.

Ketterer, M. W. (1982). Lateralized representation of affect, affect cognizance and the coronary-prone personality. *Biological Psychology, 15*, 171–189.

Kim, S. C. (1985). Family therapy for Asian Americans: A strategic-structural framework. *Psychotherapy, 22*, 342–348.

Koestler, A. (1979). *Janus: A summing up.* New York: Vintage Books.

Kohut, H. (1971). *Analysis of the self.* New York: International Universities Press.

Kohut, H. (1984). *How does analysis cure?* Chicago: University of Chicago Press.

Kolb, B., & Taylor, L. (1981). Affective behavior in patients with localized excisions: Role of lesion site and side. *Science, 214*, 89–91.

Kopp, R., Gold, L., & Pew, M. (1992). The creative imagination in psychotherapy. Presentation at the 41st North American Society of Adlerian Psychology convention, Toronto, Ontario, Canada. La Canada, CA: Audio Archives (tape).

Kosslyn, S. (1980). *Image and mind.* Cambridge, MA: Harvard University Press.

Kosslyn, S. M. (1988). Aspects of a cognitive neuroscience of mental imagery. *Science, 240*, 1621–1626.

Kosslyn, S., Holtzman, J., Farah, M., & Cazzaniga, M. S. (1985). A computational analysis of mental image generation: Evidence from functional dissociations in split-brain patients. *Journal of Experimental Psychology: General, 114*, 311–341.

Kosslyn, S., & Koenig, O. (1992). *Wet mind: The new cognitive neuroscience.* New York: The Free Press.

Kostandov, E. A., & Arzumanov, Y. L. (1986). The influence of subliminal emotional words on functional hemispheric asymmetry. *International Journal of Psychophysiology, 4*, 143–147.

Lackoff, G., & Johnson, M. (1980). *Metaphors we live by.* Chicago, IL: University of Chicago Press.

Ladavas, E., Umilta, C., Ricci-Bitti, P. E. (1980). Evidence for sex differences in right-hemisphere dominance for emotions. *Neuropsychologia, 18*, 361–366.

Langer, S. (1942/1979). *Philosophy in a new key: A study in the symbolism of reason, rite, and art.* Cambridge MA: Harvard University Press.

Lankton, C., & Lankton, S. (1989). *Tales of enchantment: Goal-oriented metaphors for adults and children in therapy.* New York: Brunner/Mazel.

Lankton, S., & Lankton, C. (1983). *The answer within: A clinical framework of Ericksonian hypnotherapy.* New York: Brunner/Mazel.

Lazarus, A. A. (1976). *Multimodal behavior therapy.* New York: Springer.

Lazarus, A. A. (1978). *In the mind's eye.* New York: Rawson.

Lazarus, A. A. (1989). *The Practice of multimodal therapy.* Baltimore: Johns Hopkins University Press.

LeShan, L. (1977). *You can fight for your life: Emotional factors in the causation of cancer.* New York: M. Evans.

Levy, J., Heller, W., Banich, M. T., & Burton, L. A. (1983). Asymmetry of perception in free viewing of faces. *Brain and Cognition, 2*, 404–419.

Lew, A., & Bettner, B. L. (1993). The Connexions Focusing Technique for using early recollections. *Individual Psychology, 49*(2), 166–184.

Ley, R. G., & Bryden, M. P. (1982). A dissociation of right and left hemispheric effects for recognizing emotional tone and verbal content. *Brain and Cognition, 1,* 3–9.

Linden, J. (1985). Insight through metaphor in psychotherapy and creativity. *Psychoanalysis and Contemporary Thought, 8*(3), 375–406.

Madanes, C. (1981). *Strategic family therapy.* San Francisco: Jossey-Bass.

Madanes, C. (1984). *Behind the one-way mirror: Advances in the practice of strategic therapy.* San Francisco: Jossey-Bass.

Malgady, R. G., & Johnson, M. G. (1976). Modifiers in metaphors: Effects of constituent phrase similarity in the interpretation of figurative sentences. *Journal of Psycholinguistic Research, 5,* 43–52.

Mann, J. (1973). *Time-limited psychotherapy.* Cambridge, MA: Harvard University Press.

Manson, S. M., & Trimble, J. E. (1982). American Indian and Alaska Native communities: Past efforts, future inquiries. In L. R. Snowden (Ed.), *Reaching the underserved: Mental health needs of neglected populations* (pp. 143–164). Beverly Hills, CA: Sage.

May, R. (1958). Contributions of existential psychotherapy. In R. May, E. Angel, & H. F. Ellenberger (Eds.), *Existence: A new dimension in psychiatry and psychology* (pp. 37-91). New York: Basic Books.

May, R. (1991). *The cry for myth.* New York: W. W. Norton.

Mayman, M. (1968). Early memories and character structure. *Journal of Projective Techniques and Personality Assessment, 32,* 303–316.

McNeill, D. (1992). *Hand and mind: What gestures reveal about thought.* Chicago: The University of Chicago Press.

Meichenbaum, D. (1977). *Cognitive-behavior modification: An integrative approach.* New York: Plenum.

Meltzoff, A., & Borton, W. (1979). Intermodal matching by human neonates. *Nature, 282,* 403–404.

Meyers, M. B., & Smith, B. D. (1987). Cerebral processing of nonverbal affective stimuli: Differential effects of cognitive and affective sets on hemispheric asymmetry. *Biological Psychology, 24,* 67–84.

Miller, A. I. (1986). *Imagery in scientific thought: Creating 20th-century physics.* Cambridge, MA: The MIT Press.

Minuchin, S., & Fishman, H. C. (1981). *Family therapy techniques.* Cambridge, Mass.: Harvard University Press.

Mosak, H. (1958). Early recollections as a projective technique. *Journal of Projective Techniques, 22*(3), 302–311.

Mosak, H., & Kopp, R. (1973). The early recollections of Adler, Freud, and Jung. *Journal of Individual Psychology, 29,* 157–166.

Murray, E., & Jacobson, L. (1978). Cognition and learning in traditional and behavioral therapy. In S. Garfield & A. Bergen (Eds.), *Handbook of psychotherapy and behavior change* (pp. 661–687). New York: Wiley.

Muslin, H. L., & Val, E. R. (1987). *The psychotherapy of the self.* New York: Brunner/Mazel.

Nash, H. (1962). Freud and metaphor. *Archives of General Psychiatry, 7,* 25–29.

Nobles, W. (1980). Extended self: Rethinking the so-called Negro self-concept. In R. L. Jones (Ed.), *Black psychology* (pp. 99–105). New York: Harper & Row.

Olson, H. (1979). *Early recollections: Their use in diagnosis and psychotherapy.* Springfield, IL: Charles C. Thomas.

Pavio, A. (1979). Psychological processes in the comprehension of metaphor. In A. Ortony (Ed.), *Metaphor and thought* (150–171). Cambridge, MA: Cambridge University Press.

Pavio, A., & Clark, J. M. (1986). The role of topic and vehicle imagery in metaphor comprehension. *Communication & Cognition, 19*, 367–387.

Perris, C. (1974). Average evoked responses (AER) in patients with affective disorders. *Acta Psychiatrica Scandinavica, Supplement, 225*, 89–98.

Perris, C. (1975). EEG techniques in the measurement of the severity of depressive syndromes. *Neuropsychobiology, 1*, 16–25.

Pribram, K. (1971). *Languages of the brain: Experimental paradoxes and principles in neuropsychology.* Englewood Cliffs, NJ: Prentice-Hall.

Pribram, K. (1978). Our brain: The holographic theory. *On the nature of reality.* Los Angeles: UCLA Extension (audiotape).

Pribram, K. (1985). What the fuss is all about. In K. Wilber (Ed.), *The holographic paradigm and other paradoxes: Exploring the leading edge of science* (pp. 27–34). Boston: New Science Library.

Pribram, K. (1990). Prolegomenon for a holonomic brain theory. In H. Haken & M. Stadler (Eds.), *Synergetics of cognition.* Berlin, Germany: Springer-Verlag.

Pribram, K. (1991). *Brain and perception: Holonomy and structure in figural processing.* New Jersey: Lawrence Erlbaum Associates.

Pribram, K. (1994). Personal communication.

Reider, N. (1972). Metaphor as interpretation. *International Journal of Psycho-Analysis, 53*, 463–469.

Ricoeur, P. (1979). The metaphorical process. In S. Sacks (Ed.), *On metaphor* (pp. 151–157). Chicago, IL: University of Chicago Press.

Ricoeur, P. (1984). *The Rule of metaphor: Multi-disciplinary studies of the creation of meaning in language.* Toronto, Ontario: University of Toronto Press.

Riechmann, P. F., & Coste, E. (1980). Mental imagery and the comprehension of figurative language. In R. R. Hoffman & R. P. Honeck (Eds.), *Cognition and figurative language* (183–200). Hillsdale, NJ: Erlbaum.

Rose, G. (1985-86). On "linguistification." *International Journal of Psychoanalytic Psychotherapy, 11*, 71–75.

Ross, E. D. (1981). The aprosodias: Functional-anatomic organization of the affective components of language in the right hemisphere. *Archives of Neurology, 38*, 561–569.

Ross, E. D., & Meuslam, M. M. (1979). Dominant language functions of the right hemisphere: prosody and emotional gesturing. *Archives of Neurology, 36*, 144–148.

Rothenberg, A. (1988). *The creative process in psychotherapy.* New York: W. W. Norton.

Segalowitz, S. J. (1983). *Two sides of the brain: Brain lateralization explored.* New York: Prentice Hall Press.

Shulman, B. (1973). *Contributions to individual psychology.* Chicago: Alfred Adler Institute.

Shulman, B., & Mosak, H. (1988). *Manual for life style assessment.* Muncie, IN: Accelerated Development.

Siegelman, E. (1990). *Metaphor and meaning in pychotherapy.* New York: The Guilford Press.

Sifneos, P. (1981). Short-term anxiety-provoking psychotherapy: Its history, technique, outcome, and instruction. In S.Budman (Ed.), *Forms of brief therapy* (pp. 45-81). New York: Guilford Press.

Silberman, E. K., & Weingartner, H. (1986). Hemispheric lateralization of functions related to emotion. *Brain and Cognition, 5*, 322–353.

Siler, T. (1987). *Metaphorms: Forms of metaphor.* New York: The New York Academy of Sciences.

Siler, T. (1990). *Breaking the mind barrier: The artscience of neurocosmology.* New York: Simon & Schuster.

Smuts, J. (1926/1961). *Holism and evolution.* New York: Viking Press.

Sperry, L. (1989). Contemporary approaches to brief psychotherapy: A comparative analysis. *Individual Psychology, 45* (nos. 1 and 2), 3–25.

Sperry, R. (1993). Sperry plumbs science for values and solutions. Interviewed by Tori DeAngelis. *American Psychological Association Monitor, 24*(6), 6–7.

Springer, S. P., & Deutsch, G. (1989). *Left brain, right brain.* New York: W. H. Freeman & Co.

Starr, A. (1977). *Rehearsal for living: Psychodrama.* Chicago: Nelson/Hall.

Stern, D. (1985). *The interpersonal world of the infant: A view from psychoanalysis and developmental psychology.* New York: Basic Books.

Strauss, E., & Kaplan, E. (1980). Lateralized asymmetries in self-perception. *Cortex, 6,* 283–293.

Strauss, S., & Moscovitch, M. (1981). Perception of facial expressions. *Brain and Language, 13,* 308–332.

Suberi, M., & McKeever, W. F. (1979). Differential right hemispheric memory storage of emotional and non-emotional faces. *Neuropsychologia, 15,* 757–768.

Sue, S. (1988). Psychotherapeutic services for ethnic minorities: Two decades of research findings. *American Psychologist, 43,* No. 4, 301–308.

Sue, S., & Zane, N. (1987). The role of culture and cultural techniques in psychotherapy. *American Psychologist, 42*(1), 37–45.

Szajnberg, N. (1985-86). Übertragung, metaphor, and transference in psychoanalytic psychotherapy. *International Journal of Psychoanalytic Psychotherapy, 11,* 53–69.

Szapocznik, J., Santisteban, D., Kurtines, W. M., Hervis, O. E., and Spencer, F. (1982). Life enhancement counseling: A psychosocial model of services for Cuban elders. In E. E. Jones & S. J. Korchin (Eds.), *Minority mental health* (pp. 296–330). New York: Praeger.

Tucker, D. M., Watson, R. T., & Heilman, K. M. (1977). Discrimination and evocation of affectively intoned speech in patients with right parietal disease. *Neurology, 27,* 947–950.

Verbrugge, R. R. (1980). Transformations in knowing: A realist view of metaphor. In R. R. Hoffman & R. P. Honeck (Eds.), *Cognition and Figurative Language* (pp. 87–126). Hillsdale, NJ: Erlbaum.

Verbrugge, R. R., & McCarrel W. S. (1977). Metaphoric comprehension: Studies in reminding and resembling. *Cognitive Psychology, 9,* 494–533.

Watzlawick, P., Weakland, J. H., & Fisch, R. (1974). *Change: Principles of problem formation and problem resolution.* New York: W. W. Norton.

Winner, E. (1988). *The point of words: Children's understanding of metaphor and irony.* Cambridge, MA: Harvard University Press.

Winner, E., & Gardner, H. (1977). The comprehension of metaphor in brain damaged patients. *Brain, 100,* 717–729.

Wolpe, J. (1958). *Psychotherapy by reciprocal inhibition.* Stanford: Stanford University Press.

Wylie, D. R., & Goodale, M. A. (1988). Left-sided oral asymmetries in spontaneous but not posed smiles. *Neuropsychologia, 26,* 823–832.

Young-Eisendrath, & Hall, J. (1991). *Jung's self psychology: A constructivist perspective.* New York: The Guilford Press.

Name Index

Subject Index